THE
PIG BUTCHERING
SCAM

How I fell for it & everything I learned

ML

DEDICATION

I give my heartfelt gratitude to all the PBS victims who found the courage to share their stories to spread public awareness in an effort to obstruct the life-destroying cyber scam industry.

Thank you to every single person in my support group who generously devoted your time and energy and selflessly shared everything you learned to help other victims move forward with life post-scam. These are some of the kindest people I have ever met, yet they are afraid to tell their stories to the news media due to the fear of humiliation and victim shaming.

I want to give special thanks to those who have inspired me to write this book through their continual words of hope and encouragement and to SM who has selflessly dedicated her time and expertise in helping me make this book a reality.

Finally, I thank GASO, all their volunteers, and all the true journalists who have selflessly risked their lives to expose the truth that most are afraid to report on. You are the heroes in the crusade to spread awareness of the PBS and fight to slow down human trafficking.

May God bless you all!

"It would never happen to me"

TABLE OF CONTENTS

INTRODUCTION

I f this is the first time you have heard of a "Pig Butchering Scam" and are curious what it is, you have come to the right place. In this book, I will be discussing what the "Pig Butchering Scam" is, dispel some myths about the kinds of people who get scammed, and share my personal story as well as a few others from members of my support group who are kind enough to share their stories. I will also discuss the psychological and emotional impact victims experience from these scams, what you can do right after discovering you have been scammed, and, most importantly, learn how to heal and move forward with your life post-scam.

For simplicity, I will, in the remainder of the book, use the abbreviation "PBS" for "Pig Butchering Scam," the word "victim" for anyone who has experienced the receiving end of the scam, regardless of how you were affected as a result of the scam, and "scammed" as a result of having been lied to and money lost through manipulation of different sorts. I want to make it clear, though, that in no way am I using the term "victim" in a demeaning, belittling, or derogatory way. This word has been so abundantly used in society that it is difficult to change or replace it. In truth, I absolutely hate to hear this term spoken because it hits home and makes me cringe when I am reminded of my experience and the financial and emotional impacts the scam had on me. Except for those who have gone public with their names, all victims in this book will be given pseudonyms due to privacy or safety concerns. Due to similar concerns, I will also keep my name and identity confidential.

As someone who had fallen prey to this type of scam, which originated in Southeast Asia and was almost unheard of here in the United States in 2021, I have come to learn a lot about human psychology, the dark side of this world that the media does not do enough to expose, as well as the human compassion that often does not receive enough attention from the media.

Furthermore, to my dismay at the time I had discovered the scam, I realized that support and resources for PBS victims was not always available. PBS victims had to devise what to do on their own. Eventually, I found and joined a newly formed support group comprised of all PBS victims residing in the United States. Although we had members from numerous states, most victims in our group resided in California, Texas, and New York. Many had lost their entire life savings and joined the group with suicidal ideation due to utter panic, devastation, fear of humiliation, and victim shaming. New to all the shock and loss, members tried to provide mutual emotional support and guidance in any way possible. We researched priorities such as what law enforcement groups we needed to report to right away or what we needed to do with our bank accounts.

In our unprecedented situation, with no clear legal framework or manual to help guide us, especially through our emotions, we were the blind leading the blind. To our surprise, many who tried to report to law enforcement, such as the local police or sheriff's department, were turned away and told there was nothing they could do to help but instead were referred to the FBI's Internet Crime Complaint Center website called "IC3." After over a year of conversing with members while gathering bits of information here and there, I decided that it would do no justice to hold the information we shared and learned within the support group alone. As a group, we feel that the information we share with each other will be helpful to unsuspecting targets who have fallen prey outside our group. Our goal is to fight the spread of the PBS by promoting awareness.

As the PBS has been spreading rapidly, yet silently, in the US in the last few years, billions of dollars have already been lost to scammers worldwide. Additionally, the manipulation that led to these enormous losses has caused severe psychological and emotional distress to the victims. About 24,000 US residents have already reported losing nearly $1 billion to these types of scams in 2021 alone.[1] Even though I am one individual, I feel defeated if I do nothing and watch the devastation spread like cancer across the US and other countries.

Prior to 2022, the topic of PBS scams had not received much publicity. When PBS does get discussed, victims are usually shamed, and the underlying psychology of the crime is ignored. Many victims are terrified and too embarrassed to show their faces on TV or in the media when sharing their stories or even use their real names. The few that have been brave enough to share their accounts with the media received backlash, mockery, and victim shaming. Many viewers or readers accused the victims of being greedy, which is far from the truth. In the Merriam-Webster dictionary, "greed" is defined as "selfish and excessive desire for more of something, such as money, than is needed."[2] Of all the stories I have heard from the hundred-plus members in our group, not one fits this definition. No victims I have talked to privately or who have told their stories publicly revealed a never-ending desire for money. Usually, these victims simply want to help others with the extra money earned through an investment. In no way have I, or any of the other victims attempted to exploit anyone to make money.

So not only have the victims suffered at the hands of the criminals, but they have suffered or are suffering from judgment and criticism from those who have heard their stories. I am saddened to see victims viewed in this way. Sophisticated psychological manipulation behind the PBS led the victims to follow the scammer's advice and make what appeared to be a legitimate investment. Shame on the so-called reporters and news media for perpetuating false narratives, recklessly blaming victims, and misusing the word "greed" as a cause of their loss. These reckless remarks do not do any justice to the victims. It is unhelpful when the media misleads the public by reporting news that has not been accurately investigated and then gives advice that has no relevance to the topic they are reporting on. For example, thoughtlessly advising the public not to give money to strangers they do not know when PBS victims believe they put money into third-party accounts registered in their name. The advice, "do not give money to people you have not met," is outdated in the PBS. True journalists and reporters have risked their lives[3] to expose the truth, while the mainstream media usually takes the easy way out by recklessly reporting what they think can gain the most clicks.

I am compelled to make it my duty to increase public awareness of this type of scam and educate the public. By writing this book, I am striving to reduce the number of those who fall prey. Unfortunately, the scammers are banking on the continued trend of victims remaining quiet and reluctant to share their experiences publicly.

I have compiled information here so that you do not have to do as much blind research as past victims have. In addition, I hope this book will provide the guidance we did not initially have, as this is still a fairly new subject matter here in the US. Although I am still in the healing process, I wish I had written this book earlier because I feel it cannot wait any longer while the scam is targeting newer victims every day.

Additionally, I am writing this book as an emotional advocate for all victims of financial scams. I want to share that, just like every other victim I know, I had always thought, "it would never happen to me," but to my shock and disbelief, it did. Therefore, I understand the shock you have experienced or are going to experience and the roller coaster of emotions you feel every day. And the doubt and diminished self-confidence after being scammed, the loss of trust in people, the blame you put on yourself for allowing this to happen, and the loss of hope because everything you had worked hard for has been stolen.

MESSAGE TO THE VICTIM

You are not alone!

If you are a victim of a scam, please know that you are definitely not alone! In the first chapter, I will reveal how underreported most scams are due to fear of humiliation and victim shaming. Furthermore, having seen how distressing the impact of being scammed can be and studying the roller coaster of emotions, I am tailoring this book to validate your emotions and provide guidance on how to navigate your life post-scam. You are not "stupid," and no, you are not "greedy." Know also that you were not scammed by one person but by a complex group working together to corner you, including software developers and psychologists. You are simply a human who has fallen prey to intentional psychological manipulation. In this book, I will also aim to dispel misconceptions about how victims get scammed.

Being a victim of a scam, especially the PBS, can be devastating and traumatizing. The heavy emotional and financial stress inevitably leads to negative thoughts about yourself. For some people, it can be unbearable and lead to suicidal thoughts and intentions. For others, the trauma can lead to chronic stress and anxiety. If you find yourself in a dark and lonely place and do not know where to go or who to turn to, please know there is help, and there is hope.

I am dedicating this book to all the victims of scams and wish to guide them back to as normal a life as possible. I want to let you know that all the roller coaster feelings you go through, no matter how trivial others may view them, are completely valid and that everyone will go through the healing process at a different pace. As Epictetus once said, what matters is "not what happens to you, but how you react to it." We must not let a series of sour events knock us down for good. Although we wish it were easier, life is full of lessons meant to strengthen us. How we deal with bad experiences will make all the difference in the world. You can either let an unfortunate event destroy your life, or you can make your life out of that event. Please know you are worthy and keep fighting on!

MESSAGE TO THE VICTIM'S FAMILY, FRIENDS, AND EVERYONE ELSE

Although I initially intended to only write this book for victims who have been scammed, I realize that limiting this book to victims would not do justice to them as they carry and hide the burden of severe emotional distress. Therefore, this book is intended for just about everyone, even including those who have shamed victims. This book aims to provide a better understanding of what goes on behind the scenes before the actual loss takes place and show that it can happen to anyone. If you are a kind, unsuspecting, compassionate human being, you may be an easy target for the perpetrator's psychological manipulation.

This book is also aimed at any family, friends, or acquaintances who know someone who has been scammed and seeks to find help and provide some source of healing. And to help them move forward to regain trust and rebuild the self-confidence that was destroyed. I urge you to listen to their stories without judgment.

If you are reading this because you are simply curious about the PBS, you will become more aware of what goes on behind the scenes of these scams and learn how elaborate and sophisticated these scams are and maybe, one day, use what you have learned to help prevent a dear family member or friend from falling prey. I thank you for having an open mind and assure you that you will feel differently and have more compassion after reading this book.

| HUMANITY DOES EXIST

A note to the victims out there: After seeing the evil side of the world through the actions of the scammers, please know that there are humans on the other side of the equation with compassion and kindness who have devoted unremitting time and energy to helping rescue victims who have been trafficked to do the scamming against their will. For example, in 2021, as the scams were unfolding at an increasing rate and victims were seeking help with almost no one to turn to, an organization called the "Global Anti-Scam Organization" (GASO) was born. This organization was founded in June 2021 by a PBS victim herself. Her vision was to provide support for victims, educate the public about the dangers of these types of scams and bring scammers to justice. The non-profit organization is run entirely by volunteers, who are all former victims of scams, in the fight to help bring justice, not only for scammed victims but also for scammers who have been trafficked and forced to perpetrate evil acts against their will. As I write this book, there are an estimated 80 volunteers devoted to helping others who have lost everything to the PBS. To fulfill its mission, GASO has been working closely with law enforcement, investigative teams, and news media worldwide. In addition, the organization has been advocating for stronger legal and institutional protections. To date, nearly 2,000 victims worldwide have contacted GASO, and it has been calculated that these victims alone have lost more than $440 million.[4] To learn more about this organization, sign up as a volunteer, or make donations, you can visit their website at www.globalantiscam.org.

Being in GASO's support group has helped me see that humanity exists. It made me look beyond what happened to me and learn from my experience to help alert others from falling prey to the PBS. And it can, in a way, also be therapeutic for me to engage in helping others. Though I have learned that you must first take care of yourself mentally and financially, you can step forward to help other victims heal and move past the trauma. It was therapeutic to know that I was not going through this alone and that many other victims have selflessly dedicated their time and efforts to support others.

I want you to know that although it may seem impossible, especially right after the discovery of the scam, it is possible to heal. The healing process will take time, but this book will help you move forward.

CHAPTER 1

THE PIG BUTCHERING SCAM (PBS)

In many ways, the advancement of technology has made our world better and improved our overall quality of life. It allows us many forms of instant gratification, such as being able to communicate faster through email or text messaging. Remember the snail mail days? Through social media and other platforms, you can instantly share any photos or thoughts you want with many people simultaneously. In addition, you can save your photos and documents to the cloud. Without having to leave home, you can bank or trade stocks online. Not only does advanced technology help make it more convenient to go about your daily life, but it has also revolutionized the workplace and made its way into the classrooms to further improve communication between teachers, administration, and students. For example, online courses and Zoom meetings became common during the Covid-19 lockdowns.

Although technology was designed to improve our world, it has its downsides and potential risks. Besides the obvious real-life social disconnect and decreased level of physical activity, there are concerns about user privacy and data security. While technology makes it easy for the user to go about their daily business, it also attracts the dangers of criminals seeking to steal your data. Furthermore, cyberbullying has claimed lives. Online scams have ruined lives. Scammers have become adept at using new technology to their benefit. Cybercriminals can search the internet for current trends, create fake accounts, and impersonate legitimate companies to steal information and money from you.

There are many kinds of scams that we have been trained to watch out for, whether we were warned by the news media, government websites, or the workplace. Most scams traditionally target seniors. You've also heard about many common scams, such as identity theft, IRS or government imposters, telemarketing, random texts, or phishing. You've also heard about employment, online shopping, sweepstakes, lottery, charity, psychic, inheritance, counterfeit check, debt relief, Nigerian prince or advance fee, romance, mortgage, rental, investment, Ponzi scheme, recovery, or senior phone scams.

If sufficiently educated, we are able to avoid these common scams. We have been trained never to click on links from texts or emails from senders we do not know, even if they draw a sense of urgency or threat. Even if you know the sender, we have been cautioned never to download any attachments since your contact's account may have been hacked. And we know not to click on links from emails that seem to appear from legitimate businesses, such as your bank, even if you see the official logo.

We know the best action is to go to the company website through their secure address.

We are warned never to download untrusted or unverified apps or websites since we might risk downloading a virus and spyware alongside. We have been reminded never to share personal information or give money to strangers. We have been trained to never provide any confidential information, such as a credit card or social security number, over the phone or in person to any unknown person because they may be posing as a legitimate entity to steal your information. We have been alerted to pay attention to ATM or point of sale (POS) machines and be suspicious of any signs of tampering.

As we know, some scams may be more complex than others. With its unimaginable complexity, the PBS takes the cake. Investment scams such as those from the PBS can be sophisticated and insidious. Once it had been driven out of China due to growing public awareness and hence becoming less effective there, this so-called "super scam" expanded after 2020 primarily as a knock-on effect of the economic ruin caused by the Covid-19 pandemic. And with the need to make use of newly constructed casinos that have laid vacant in Southeast Asia, crime syndicates adapted to the circumstances by tricking forced labor into carrying out their crimes.[1]

Perversely, a combination of advances in blockchain technology (such as Bitcoin becoming the first cryptocurrency in 2009, while Ethereum was released in 2015, and machine or deep learning making great advances in 2016, which automated coherent translation from Chinese to other languages via Google Translate) enabled this new incarnation of international crime. The buzz surrounding cryptocurrencies, combined with the normalization of new social connections established online during the Covid-19 pandemic and the overall isolation caused by the ensuing lockdowns in much of the US, paved the way for a perfect combination of events that coincided to give rise to this new super scam.

In this chapter, I will elaborate on the PBS, an investment scam almost unheard of here in the US only a couple of years ago. I will expose and discuss in detail how the PBS masterminds use social engineering, classic persuasion, and emotional manipulation techniques, alongside cryptocurrency trading, to steal enormous sums of money from unsuspecting victims. To better understand how the PBS played out recently, I will also discuss the history behind it.

Additionally, by sharing my account of falling for the scam and a few stories from our GASO support group members, I hope this book will shed more light on how no PBS is identical, but also by learning the similar tactics that scammers have used to successfully lure and manipulate the victims, you will be better prepared to spot red flags should you ever become a target. Before I begin, let me reveal some recent yet staggering statistics on the wealth lost as a result of these scams.

STATISTICS

I will share some statistics as a window into the financial impact that scams have worldwide and how underreported they are in the news, media, and other sources. Prompted by the emergence of Covid-19 and the ensuing lockdowns, financial scams became more prevalent, and investment fraud rose to record levels in 2021. According to GASO, cybercrime is now a multi-million-dollar industry in Southeast Asia (SEA), ruining tens of thousands of lives around the world.[2] To fuel these labor-intensive criminal enterprises, the scamming industry created a secondary industry of human trafficking with hundreds of thousands of workers trapped and forced to fulfill their masterminds' desires. In 2021, scam companies from SEA netted $429 million from 4,325 PBS victims in the US alone.[3] However, tens of billions of USD worth of cryptocurrency are reported to have been stolen by the SEA companies. In China, the original target market of the SEA crime syndicates, 40 billion RMB was stolen in 2020 from the PBS alone.

According to the Federal Trade Commission (FTC), in 2021, romance scam victims got hit with a record of $547 million in losses which was an 80% increase compared to 2020 and six times the losses reported in 2017.[4] With more than $1 billion of losses reported in 2021 by 46,000 victims, the financial damages caused by crypto-related scams have increased 60-fold over the past three years.[5] What's more, the Consumer Financial Protection Bureau (CFPB) reported that, between October 2018 and September 2022, about 40% of over 8,300 total crypto-related complaints were related to fraud, with the PBS and other romance scams in the lead.[6] Beyond the US, staggering financial losses due to crypto romance scams have been reported in numerous countries within Asia, Europe, Oceania, and elsewhere. The PBS's success lies in its lack of geographic boundaries, which allows for seemingly endless expansion.

According to the Global Anti-Scam Alliance (GASA), only 7% of PBS victims report their financial losses.[7] Therefore, based on this estimate of extremely low reporting, the numbers of unreported crimes are much higher. Due to shame, guilt, embarrassment, and victim shaming, it is estimated that only about 15% of fraud victims in the United States report their crimes to law enforcement and because of these same reasons, most never disclose their loss to family or friends.[8] Contrary to the stereotype of the typical scam victim, most PBS victims are highly educated, with about 88% having either an undergraduate or post-graduate degree. Though highly educated and sophisticated in their understanding of technology, these victims are still vulnerable to the brute force psychological manipulation techniques used by the PBS masterminds. The enduring psychological damage caused by the PBS is substantial. To date, according to one estimate, at least five US victims of the PBS have seen no alternative to the social and financial ruin and have taken their own lives.

In addition to the social shame and psychological damage, victims face extraordinary financial setbacks. This theft enabled by crypto allows enormous sums of money to be transferred to criminal wallets at record speed, making the scale of this international theft unprecedented. According to a survey GASO collected from 550 victims as of July 6, 2022, about 33% of PBS victims report being in debt post-scam, while 77% emptied their savings. In addition, a reported 43% of victims have borrowed from friends or family and 39% sold off stocks and retirement funds.[9] With retirement once planned with confidence, these victims now face a precarious future.

And yet, with nihilistic joy, the cybercriminals in northern Myanmar responsible for ruining and sometimes taking lives will set off fireworks for every $500k USD scammed.[10] Across Myanmar, Cambodia, Laos, the Philippines, Malaysia, Thailand, and, more recently, Dubai, this professionalized criminal activity ruthlessly brings in high returns that bosses are happy to celebrate.

| THE PBS OVERVIEW

Originating in China, these scams were first known as Shāzhūpán (or Sha Zhu Pan, 杀猪盘) Chinese term which has been more recently translated as "Pig Butchering Scam" as it made its way to Western countries, mainly the United States.[1,2] The PBS has also been referred to as Crypto Romance Scam or Hybrid Investment Romance Scam.[2] Unlike most of the scams I have mentioned, the PBS is carried out on a sophisticated, highly-organized, and shockingly industrialized scale, with many perpetrators involved in carrying out each individual scam.

According to the GASO website, there are now about five types of PBS[2]:

1) Fake investment websites and apps

2) Fake brokers on Meta Trader 4 and 5
3) Fake liquidity mining pools
4) Group investments
5) Gambling

Due to knowledge acquired through personal experience, I will primarily discuss the crypto scam that involves fake investment websites and apps. To encapsulate this chapter in one short sentence, the PBS is analogous to raising a pig, fattening it up, and then butchering it when it reaches its prime stage.

The PBS strategy begins with the predator scouring social media such as Facebook, Instagram, and LinkedIn or dating websites such as Hinge, OkCupid, Tinder, or Coffee Meets Bagel to identify potential targets. This long con focuses first on seemingly innocuous relationship-building, typically involving some type of romance until the predator convinces the targets to better plan their future via a fraudulent crypto investment scheme. To attract potential targets, they first create a profile using stolen photos (purchased for as little as $3-$4 on Chinese social media platforms like WeChat to prevent reverse-image search[3]) of handsome men or beautiful women. The profile will include impressive credentials such as graduating from a prestigious university or majoring in finance. Their hobbies will typically include that they like to travel and enjoy reading or following economics.

The predators will always portray themselves as financially well-off yet loving and kind souls who are very giving. They will share stolen photos or short video recordings of charity events they supposedly contributed to, their supposed pets, children, home, car, or workplace. They will send pictures of their food, usually always restaurant quality, to draw more interest from their targets and reinforce familiarity. They will pretend to live near you or come from the same place you were raised. They may also pretend to be in the same industry as you. This is the classic persuasion technique of "liking and similarity," which slowly primes the target to make them more susceptible to agreeing to future fake investment.[4] The predator will then reveal their past love life, which had a traumatic ending, such as a partner blatantly cheating on them or dying in a car crash a few years prior. This will manipulate the target's emotions to trigger feelings of sympathy. The predator will say that, although it took a while, they have moved on and are now ready to start a new life with someone special. They will thank the heavens that fate brought them to meet on the dating app or social media platform.

Even if the target is not immediately interested in building a relationship with the predator, who is continually guided by a carefully crafted script tailored across personality types, backgrounds, and interests, the predator uses persuasion to keep them engaged and interested.[4,5] For example, one of the predator's favorite topics is their "uncle," a financial analyst who has mentored them for years. The uncle taught them the "secrets" to investing in cryptocurrency that will help boost their savings and enable early retirement. The predator is banking on the likelihood that the target does not know much about cryptocurrency and will pretend that he or she can be their mentor using the knowledge and secrets learned from their "uncle." As the predator attempts to build an intimate relationship with the victim, they are said to be "raising the pig."

Since the PBS criminals work in teams with an intentional division of labor to make the best use of the criminal "talent," the target will first interact with a lower-level scammer seeking to generate leads. As a casual aside (never presented as the main focus), the predator will mention to the victim that they have been watching the market and will send a screenshot of a complicated candlestick trading chart. If the victim demonstrates interest in "learning" to invest, they will eventually be handed off to a higher-level predator who is more experienced with emotional manipulation and can take the "lead" to the next level. At this time, there may be a trade-off to the more experienced predator, and the phone may disconnect momentarily. Shortly after, the victim will be transferred to an encrypted messaging platform such as WhatsApp or Telegram.

The predator then proceeds with grooming their target by being excellent listeners (asking lots of questions while carefully planning which emotional "buttons to push" in the coming weeks) and demonstrating persistent care and concern through daily communication. The predator slowly trains the target by delivering seemingly innocent "good morning" and "good night" texts with kiss emojis like clockwork (at 8 a.m. and 10:00 p.m. each day). This both trains the target to become emotionally dependent and to respond automatically to the predator's cues (instinctive response). Throughout the day, they ask their targets if they have gotten enough sleep or rest, food to eat, or water to replenish themselves. This polite and attentive behavior will encourage the target to lower their guard and slowly transition them into a childlike, helpless state of mind that is easier to control. Within about two weeks, the predator will first confess love and then start to use "flirty" pet names such as "daddy" for the predator and "babe," "baby," or, less frequently, "wife" for the target. This familial language instills trust and further pushes the victim into an easily manipulated, childlike state of mind. Most of the time, the predator will act like they are busy with their work or other important responsibilities to show their targets they are hardworking and responsible with their jobs or family affairs.

The predator will groom their target for a few weeks and earn their trust through the use of carefully crafted language. They will repeatedly use the words "trust," "love," and "happy" for a hypnotic effect that is strengthened by the animated GIFs (😊 , 😊 , 😊 , Peach and Goma kissing, etc.) and infinite scroll that are built into messaging apps such as WhatsApp and Telegram. The weeks of repetition establish a sense of constant companionship, convincing the targets that the predator genuinely cares and wants to help them build a better financial future. According to the predator, this better future will be achieved by guiding the victim through the ins and outs of cryptocurrency investment. Once the target has been sufficiently persuaded, the predator will ultimately lure their targets to open an account on a professional-looking fraudulent platform.

To successfully persuade the target to "invest," the predator first guides them to open an account with a legitimate cryptocurrency exchange platform such as Coinbase, Binance, Kraken, or Crypto.com, where the victim will convert their money to cryptocurrency (usually USDT, to "offset risk"). The predator is presented as an infinitely patient and nurturing "teacher," with helpful screenshots intended to guide the victim through each step of the process. Appeals to authority are used to reinforce trust, with comments like "Coinbase is a legitimate cryptocurrency exchange in the United States, which is protected by the federal government." Next, the predator guides the target to download a popular app, such as Meta Trader, through Google's Android or Apple's App Store, when it was available for the PBS that occurred in 2021-22.[6]

In other cases, the predator will insist that Coinbase Wallet be used to "trade in the secondary market." The target will be guided to use the Coinbase Wallet's browser to access a professionally simulated fraudulent platform, which requires the user to upload their ID to create an account and where the user creates their own password for account "protection." Once the account is created, the user can chat with the 24-hour customer service anytime to facilitate "reloading" the account balance and for any other support questions.

The predator, while also showing the target the same app he or she is using and how much money he or she has been making, then "teaches" the target how to use both platforms. The predator encourages their target to invest "together" for mutual interest when it comes to their financial future. During the entire process of opening and creating their own "investment" account, the targets believe that their money is under their own name and is entirely under their control. At this point, the victim will be so accustomed to following step-by-step instructions from their loving and patient "teacher" that they will barely notice the red flags present in the fraudulent website's design. Even when the victim sees the red flags on an intellectual level, cognitive dissonance takes over, and it feels impossible that such a good-natured, polite, and loving friend could be untrustworthy.

The predator then politely urges the target to first make a small "test" deposit which will be (unbeknownst to the target) sent to a criminal wallet address. The transaction is prompted by a sense of urgency that is created when the predator explains, "I just don't want you to miss the market because it doesn't happen every day. Maybe it's over in a few days, or maybe it's a year away." At this stage, the target has unwittingly become a victim and is the "pig" being "raised" and prepared to be "fattened" by the perpetrator.[2]

Although the victim is still skeptical, the perpetrator calms their fear of the unknown by walking the victim through each step of the process, including showing them how to view their recent transactions and account balance, which typically reflects an already high amount. As the perpetrator shows the victims how their money can grow through fake simulations that emulate the real market, the victim becomes more comfortable with the trading process. The perpetrator will then encourage or suggest that the victim withdraw their money as a way of testing the platform to convince them that what they are working with is real. Through a series of more motivating conversations and building confidence with the victim through the availability of the

24-hour customer service, the scammer then lures the victim to put in more money to build up or "fatten" their accounts. They advise the victims to use the concept of "borrowing more chicken to lay more eggs" to encourage the victims to borrow money from family and friends or to take out personal loans, which, according to the perpetrator, is regarded as standard in the field of investments. Throughout the process, the perpetrator never asks the victim for personal information such as a bank account number or user password since the account supposedly belongs to the victim.

As the perpetrator continues to pressure the victim to deposit larger sums of money into their account to make higher-yield trades and "capture this great market," the victim will share that they can no longer "invest" anymore, and their bank accounts are now empty. The victim will express concerns about the platform when they are requested to pay a hefty tax (about 20%-35% of the deposit combined with fake "earnings") or a penalty for "early" withdrawal. The scammer will create a sense of urgency for the victim to "invest" more money as soon as possible, claiming that otherwise, they will lose everything. Once the victim expresses concern that they can no longer "invest" any more money and becomes suspicious of the fraudulent platform, as well as the person they once thought was a true friend, the victim again expresses their desire to withdraw all their money.

At this stage, some victims may fall prey to the simulated tax and early withdrawal fees and be told afterward that they have to pay an endless series of fees until they have no money left. Others will reveal to the scammer that they are aware they have been scammed. The scammer will use any remaining leverage to persuade the victims to take out loans to pay their "taxes" or early withdrawal fee. When the victim says they have no savings left and cannot take out more loans, this is the final stage in the scam where the perpetrator and his/her team go in for the "butchering" or "killing." The scammers behind the scenes may display a message on their website that an upgrade is coming to give the victim no reason to worry that their money will disappear. The platform is no longer accessible, so the victim is no longer able to see their account nor able to contact the 24-hour customer service. Typically, at this point, the scammers will either disappear or play along and pretend not to know why the website is not working. Some will play the victim and pretend to also be in trouble if confronted. Others will blame the victim for getting themselves into the mess. At this point, all money will have been sent to a criminal cryptocurrency wallet: the "pig" has been "butchered." The "butchering" usually happens on a Friday as the scammers use the long weekend to their advantage, knowing you are unlikely able to reach anyone who could do anything over the weekend to help you while they continue to launder your money to their final destinations.

Regardless of how fast the victim reports the crime, the funds are usually laundered away right after the victims transfer money to what they thought was their own personal account. Although news reports have shown PBS happening in China since 2016, it was realized that when this scheme exploded in 2019, millions of dollars had already been stolen from victims.[7] Although there was little information available about these scams before 2019, outside of news from the Chinese-language media, these scams were believed to be widespread in China until the Covid-19 pandemic hit and lockdowns persisted in China until 2022. Unbeknownst to the rest of the world, the lockdowns and tighter regulations, combined with China's unprecedented call for its nationals to return home in 2021, provoked a new twist to these scams. Although the PBS slowed down in China due to tighter government regulations, it moved on to target Chinese speakers in Southeast Asia. And with advanced translation technology available (via Google Translate), the PBS quickly spread beyond the Chinese-speaking world. Furthermore, what initially began with grooming victims to place bets on fake gambling websites and later becoming known as a romance-oriented investment scam, the PBS recently expanded into cultivating more professional, business-oriented relationships.[7]

To better understand how the PBS exploded in recent years, we need to investigate what was happening during the Covid-19 pandemic. According to an article by the United States Institute of Peace (USIP),[11] there were already plans in place by the Chinese Triad cartels and crime syndicates to conduct illegal gambling activities in nearby countries where certain remote and criminal zones were unregulated, just a few years prior to the emergence of Covid-19. Billions of dollars had already been poured into building casinos in these unregulated areas in the hopes of attracting local Chinese gamblers and tourists. Corrupt countries such as Laos and Cambodia were reported to have proliferated in these types of criminal zones as local officials and elites had often helped promote these criminal activities in the unregulated areas.

The economic fallout resulting from the pandemic motivated migrants to seek work in these countries when enticed by job offers with high pay and great benefits. Many recruits were foreigners from nearby countries including China, Taiwan, Malaysia, Thailand, Vietnam, and Hong Kong.[9,10]

However, Myanmar, a country adjacent to China previously known as "Burma," has been especially active with its criminal zone activities. While it has been reported that between 50,000 to 100,000 recruits were lured in by crime syndicates and forced to work in slave-like conditions in Cambodia, Myanmar was reported to have as many as three times more people who were also deceived and lured in by social media with enticing job offers. Due to the newly built casinos sitting vacant and not attracting local Chinese gamblers and tourists due to Covid-19 restrictions, they had to find creative methods to make up for the lost billions of anticipated revenues that never materialized.[11] To recoup the billions spent to erect the casinos, they invented a new scam. They decided to use a different method to bring in fraudulent income remotely. This new method relied heavily on exploiting human labor to carry out online cryptocurrency scams. This created a new humanitarian crisis that may come as shocking news to many outside of Southeast Asia. It is the birth of modern human slavery on an industrial scale, created and abetted by social media and the hype for cryptocurrency.

The scam companies emotionally manipulate their recruits, and according to Taiwanese news media, ring leaders will do what they can to easily control them, including giving them sleeping pills. The recruits work in teams, all lodged inside secret compounds. They are taught psychological warfare and have regular team meetings and progress reports. According to Forbes, each recruit is handed multiple mobile phones so that they are able to easily talk to multiple targets daily. Team members can rotate to talk to the same target daily. Those who meet their targets are rewarded, while those who fail or try to escape are usually tortured, abused, deprived of food, or sold to other gangs or criminal syndicates. We have heard stories of human trafficking victims who do not see the light of day or even get three meals per day. There have also been reports of murder and suicidal ideation.[10]

Regardless of the relationship type, most of the scammers are captives working against their will and, therefore, mostly victims themselves. They have been forcefully trained by relentless bosses to build relationships over an extended length of time, to gain the target's trust before they persuade or convince them to invest. There are varied methods to lure and groom the targets (scripts are varied, perfected with A/B testing, and tailored to every personality type). Once the target is sufficiently persuaded and agrees to venture into a "better future" by agreeing to invest, the target enters into a world of teams of multiple scammers trained to accomplish one thing: fatten up their pig before going in for the slaughter.

Although the PBS has been more commonly known as a romance scam aimed at dating sites and targeting lonely singles, it has evolved over the past few years to target anyone, whether single or married, lonely or content. Many targets have been victimized outside of dating sites on various platforms, including LinkedIn,

Facebook, Instagram, WhatsApp, Telegram, Line, and WeChat. Because it originated in China, the early targets were Chinese speakers living outside China because of the comfort of common language and culture. But with translation apps like Google Translate now using deep neural networks to deliver quality translations from Chinese for free,[12] scammers have advanced to English, German, French, and Spanish-speaking targets. They will attack any ethnic group as long as they have the language tools to communicate with the targets.

Experiencing this scam has opened my eyes to the appalling state of modern human trafficking and criminal networks in Southeast Asia. I am grateful, however, that what had been unknown to Westerners for a long time has been uncovered and shared by USIP[11] and Al Jazeera English[13] as well as some brave journalists and organizations who dedicate their lives to exposing these crimes. I applaud the journalism from people such as Cyrus Farivar at Forbes, Alastair McCready at Vice, and Cezary Podkul at ProPublica for exposing this criminal industry to the rest of the world so that we can all be aware of this 21st century humanitarian crisis. I also applaud GASO for their dedicated work in collecting evidence from PBS victims, as well as scammers who were victims of human trafficking desperately reaching out to them for help. Without GASO's massive influence and efforts, we would not have seen so many stories in the media about these atrocities still brewing in Southeast Asia.

As I was writing my story, I told members of my support group of my endeavor to help spread awareness, and a few kind and brave victims allowed me to share their stories as well. Like me, they did not feel comfortable holding their own experience inside and wanted to share their experiences to increase awareness.

By the time you finish reading these stories, you will see a pattern and notice the red flags throughout. However, if you were in our shoes and had not heard of these stories, you too might have been caught off-guard. The persuasion and emotional manipulation techniques used by the PBS criminals are powerful if they hit you at the right place and time and would work on anyone who is not familiar with this type of scam. Therefore, I am sharing these stories with the hope of preventing others from falling prey to the PBS or any other type of scam. Awareness is crucial for prevention.

(Next up is my story)

| MY STORY

Curiosity killed the cat

I admit that this part of the book is, by far, the most challenging for me to write. I tried hard to wipe out this memory because of how traumatizing it was to recall how I lost my entire life savings. Having to relive my nightmare to tell my story is painful. However, because I feel that it is important to share my story to spread further awareness of the PBS and the psychological tactics used to "raise," "fatten," and "butcher" the victims, I will set aside my trepidation to do so. Regrettably, due to embarrassment and fear of possible retaliation from scammers, I will need to remain anonymous as I describe my experience. This will include my profession and total amount lost.

I do not feel that my case is similar to the ones that were featured in the news, media, or other articles. I did not feel I was in a vulnerable state at the time the whole scam began to unfold, or greedy for money. I was actually in a content state of mind and mood the year and month that I got scammed. It was summertime, the sun was shining, and I was feeling happy. I spent a good amount of my summer days enjoying the outdoors. I was healthy and in good physical and mental shape. I have young children who are also generally happy, healthy, and loving, and I am constantly surrounded by family and friends. As an essential worker, I had a stable job that was not affected by the Covid-19 pandemic. I was financially secure and able to support myself and my large family. I was feeling good at the time because I had also saved a substantial amount of money for my kids' college funds, emergency savings for rainy days, and a down payment for a new home. I could not have been happier in 2021. Everything seemed to be going well. I was cheery that season when I saw baby birds born in a nest built on my door. I thought to myself that this might be my lucky year. In Chinese superstition, the presence of a bird's nest being built in your home is a sign of good luck. It is supposed to represent life, growth, health, love, and good karma returning to you, which many people have told me would come my way. I thought everything was going to be great.

However, on July 5th, 2021, I made a fateful decision that would forever change my life. Like many during the Covid-19 lockdown, I stayed home when I was not at work and started to spend time online. My horror story began when I decided to go onto Facebook after a long absence. I wasn't looking for anyone or anything in particular. I just wanted to browse because I was single and curious. I had already been divorced for a few years and had not gone online for a long time while being busy with work and family. I thought maybe I should take this extra time in the lockdown to start looking and see who else was out there. Because we were in the middle of the Covid-19 pandemic, it was not ideal to meet anyone in person. I thought getting to know people online first would be a good idea. I was not in a rush to form a relationship, but I was curious. However, to search profiles, you have to create your own account. I created one and swiped past hundreds of profiles, but one stood out. The profile was attractive and professional-looking, and I wondered why a person this handsome would be on a dating site? Is he the type that likes to mingle with multiple people at the same time? Why isn't he taken? Curious, I decided to go ahead and click on the "like" button to find out more. It didn't take long for that person to like me back, and after a few messages, he asked me to switch to WhatsApp to continue talking. I had never used WhatsApp, but I knew it is a popular messaging app owned by Facebook (now Meta). After downloading WhatsApp, I noticed most of the contacts saved to my phone were already using it. Quickly switching to an encrypted messaging platform like WhatsApp should have been the first red flag, but my polite new friend gave me no reason to be suspicious.

What got my guard down was I was in no hurry to respond to this person because we were only starting to get to know each other. This person did not ask anything unusual, but the typical get-to-know-you kind of questions such as, "what do you do for a living?," "what are your future plans?," etc. He was polite and sincere about his interest in getting to know me. I thought it was nice that he would then start to check in with me daily with morning greetings to see if I had enough rest and evenings to see if I got home from work safely.

Within a few days, my new friend mentioned that he wanted to buy a home and asked if I had any advice on buying a house. According to his profile, he lived not too far from me. He stated he was renting in Irvine, California but was considering buying a house in Beverly Hills. He said he had saved enough money to buy a home with cash since he didn't believe in owing the bank money. Again, I did not notice anything unusual about this conversation. Because most people who live in Irvine are highly educated and earn a good income, it did not come as a surprise that he would be able to save enough money to purchase a home with cash. In the past two decades, I had heard of and competed with many people trying to buy homes with only cash. To continue the conversation, I asked how much he had saved, and he said about $2 million. That's when he told me he had a secret that he shares with the few people who are most important to him. For security reasons, I will give this "new friend" the pseudonym of HT.

HT said that during the Covid-19 pandemic, when a lot of people were losing their jobs, he had a business that was doing well, and he was not financially affected by the pandemic. He presented himself as a hardworking and intelligent professional and even shared his knowledge about the solar business. As an aside, he shared that he was thriving during the pandemic as a result of his investment in cryptocurrency. HT described how he had "mastered" his skills with trading bitcoin futures contracts because he has been doing it since 2018. He said he does not invest in stocks because the profits are too small and slow and that he does not hold bitcoin because that is risky. He stated that, with bitcoin futures contracts, no matter how unstable the market is, you usually get a return that is around 10%. He described the trades as "short-term contracts" and warned that there is not a good opportunity every day, so you must seize every opportunity and plan every step. Since I was curious from hearing all the hype about crypto and seeing ads everywhere, I was all ears even though I was hesitant to invest. Although I did not tell him, I had been secretly wanting to learn about crypto and didn't want to be left behind. Of course, I had never ventured in that direction because I did not know anyone who knew enough about investing in crypto to teach me. Due to fear of missing out (FOMO), I thought it would be good to learn something new. And, for a brief moment, the temptation of joining the FIRE movement (financial independence/retire early) flashed across my mind. The idea of this movement is to be able to afford to live your life, living on your own terms and not on an employer's. Early retirement is a natural desire because humans require a sense of agency (and a strong locus of control) to live fulfilling lives. However, I still did not want to admit to HT that I was interested in learning crypto.

Eventually, I let my guard down and soon was manipulated into believing that it would be a wise decision to learn how to earn extra income to better support my family. The thought that I would not have to worry about taking out loans to purchase a home or send my kids to college was appealing. I was manipulated into believing that I was smart enough to make the best decisions for my children and give them a better life by not allowing opportunities such as crypto investment to slip me by. I would be able to take care of my family without worries with the profit I would make.

Somehow, HT just knew all the right things to say even though I let him know I wasn't interested or ready to learn it yet. He was very patient and never pressured me into anything. However, he would reveal to me that he is planning for his future so that he can take good care of his future wife and family. He told me the sob story of how his ex-girlfriend cheated on him while they were apart during his business trip, but a few years have passed, and he is now ready to move on. He even said it must be by fate that we had met online and thanked the heavens for making us cross paths. He shared his plans about retiring early with the profits from his investment. In an attempt to create a romantic setting, he offered to teach me so that we would have common interest and therefore be able to later enjoy life together through our common interests. He said he would teach me how to do the basics while he does the more complicated stuff, like studying when to do the transactions and when we should buy up or down. He stated he has been doing this for years and uses software that helps him predict the market pretty accurately. He had also mentioned earlier that he had taken his "uncle" to the "market" and then showed me a picture of the profit his uncle made and asked if I wanted to learn. Knowing that I was not immediately interested, he tried to convince me by suggesting that I make a small deposit to begin with. He recommended starting with around $4k so that I can dip my feet in and learn how it works. As I see my money grow and become comfortable enough with the process, I can then put in more money and continue to watch it grow.

Once I was convinced to give it a try, he instructed me to download the Coinbase app. Since Coinbase was a legitimate American company based out of San Francisco and advertises itself as a "secure online platform for buying, selling, transferring and storing cryptocurrency," I felt comfortable enough to use the app. By mid-July, I put in my first deposit of $4k to Coinbase. HT then instructed me to go to the app store on my phone to download the one for the investment platform that I will be doing trading on. I informed him that I could not find the app he suggested on my Android phone. He responded by letting me know he thought I was using an Apple iPhone and was not sure if the company app would be available to use on my Android phone. Since I couldn't find the app for that trading company, he provided a link to the investment platform he was currently using. I didn't think anything of it at the time since I don't always use apps to go to a legitimate company's website. For example, instead of using a bank app, I would log on to the website directly to do my online banking. To continue, I converted my money on Coinbase from US dollars to USDT and transferred my funds to the investment platform to do all my trading and transactions. Because Coinbase charges excessive transaction fees, I trusted that those fees were collected to conduct legal transactions and validate all transactions before money would leave their platform. Furthermore, when I researched the website that I would be doing the trading on, I did not see any immediate red flags either. The trading company was registered in the state of Colorado with an Entity ID# and was listed in good standing. Because this company was registered in the United States, I trust that it had gone through some type of application screening in order for it to obtain a legal business permit and maintain its good status. However, I realize now how naïve I was to trust that just because you're licensed as a business in the United States doesn't mean it will be a legitimate business or has gone through any rigorous screening, or shockingly, any real screening whatsoever. So little did I know that the investment platform he was going to have me send money to via Coinbase was actually a complete scam company. Again, my bad for thinking that a legitimate company like Coinbase would only allow transactions with legal companies. I had no reason to be suspicious that Coinbase was willing to do business with just any company as long as they profited from each transaction that I and their so-called protected consumers would make. I had no idea that there were such things as fake exchanges for investment trading doing transactions with legitimate US companies like Coinbase.

Furthermore, everything on the fake platform looked extremely real and professional. They had a 24hr customer service team available to answer any questions through their chat function. To earn my trust at the beginning, HT offered me the option to withdraw some money to make sure I am comfortable with using the platform. By doing so, he displayed that he was doing his job in teaching me the basics so that I would feel confident and that there was nothing to worry about because the platform was real. I had decided that if he had offered to teach me how to withdraw, he wanted me to earn his trust and be comfortable with his teaching skills. However, the thought of having to pay taxes after each withdrawal seemed like a headache, so I decided to bypass the option of early withdrawal. I was thinking that I will withdraw all my money out sometime in the next few weeks once I learn how to do a few more transactions and make a little extra income. I did not plan on keeping my money on the platform for long as I was worried about the future stability of the market.

By the end of July, after two weeks of trading which were only done on some of the "good" days, HT would show me a screenshot of his current balance. He tried to emphasize the point that the more you make and the more you put in, you can maximize your profit on an even larger scale. As he showed me how the money could grow by trading, he also encouraged me to communicate with the 24hr customer service team to see if they are or will be running any promotions. In the back of my mind, I was beginning to get skeptical once he mentioned promotion. But I messaged the chat team anyway to see what their response would be. Of course, they had a promotion going on. They offered different tiers of benefits. Per HT's suggestion, I foolishly replied that I was interested in the promotion on their lowest tier, which was if you put in $500k you would receive a $100k bonus. I was thinking this could be done over time if you continued to do the trading and used the profits toward meeting the requirement. I also thought, since I have sufficient money in my savings and retirement account that I could borrow some from there and return them back to my original account within 30 days.

Once customer service received my reply showing interest, I was shocked to find out that I was automatically locked in to complete their challenge. I thought that, by expressing interest, I would be able to ask some more questions and learn more about their promotions. After a few inquiries and exchanges with the customer service team, I realized that the time frame they decided to set to complete the challenge was nearly impossible for me to complete. I had only 10 days. Where would I find the money to put in in such a short period of time? When I initially let customer service know I was interested, I did not know about the short time frame and did not realize by expressing interest that I would be automatically locked in to their "challenge."

When I tried to back out, explaining that I would not be able to complete the challenge on time, I was informed that they had already submitted my request and the "seat" has already been reserved for me. They stated they cannot reverse the request because the challenge was transferred to and handled by a different department which they do not have control over. Their job was to submit the requests only. When I questioned what would happen if I could not meet the requirement, they informed me my account would be frozen unless I paid an excessive fee to unlock it. Once my account is unlocked, I would be able to continue my trading. However, I would still have to commit to completing the challenge. That was when I had the horrible gut feeling that I may have gotten scammed. However, that feeling was briefly brushed under the rug when HT shared that he had just signed up for the promotion on the second tier, which required him to put in 1 million to get a much higher bonus. HT suggested contacting customer service to see if they could extend the deadline for me. I followed his suggestion, and per my request, customer service informed me they would be able to extend it by only a few days without any penalty.

HT then made another suggestion of borrowing money from family and friends to be able to successfully complete the challenge. He introduced to me the concept of "borrowing a chicken to lay eggs." He explained that when you borrow money, you would be able to make more, so when you have the extra income, you should be able to easily repay the borrowed money and even consider giving a bonus as a "thank you" gift to your family and friends you had borrowed from. Later on, I found his thinking to be in accordance with this article I read by NBOX.[1] The article stated that borrowing a chicken to lay eggs is the standard in the field of investment.[1] I was very hesitant to do anything like that, but he assured me when everything is done in the two weeks' time frame, I should be able to get all my money back, so there is really nothing to worry about when it comes to borrowing money.

To distract my mind from thinking that I was scammed, HT revealed his plan to borrow money from his mom and business partner to complete his challenge. When I informed him that I did not have any family and friends to borrow from, he replied: "no pressure, but you need to come up with a way to find the money to complete the challenge." He first offered to help me fulfill the challenge once he received his money back but later suggested that I try to figure out where or how I could get the rest of my money to fulfill the challenge.

Once HT completed the challenge, he stated that according to customer service, he should be able to receive his money back in 7-10 business days. I held out looking for additional funds to fulfill my challenge as I waited to see if he had received his money back yet. After one week, he informed me that there would be a delay in receiving his money and that he may not receive it until after my deadline had passed. He said he would try really hard to find a way to help me out. He even suggested selling a house that he owns in China, but due to the short time frame, he may be risking a huge loss and possibly only receive half of the value of the home. He asked if he helped me out, would I be able to pay him back right away? I told him that was a silly question because if I borrowed his money, of course, I would pay him back, but the soonest that could happen would be right after I received the full funds from my withdrawal.

When I brought up the concern if this trading company could be scamming us, he replied that he chooses to believe that everything is real and not think about the possibility of losing all the money he had already invested in. He even assured me that he had completed the same challenge some months ago and received his money back very smoothly without any issues. So, I thought to myself, if indeed this was a scam, then there's an equal chance that he might also not be able to receive his money back from the same company. Since he shared that he was willing to risk losing money by selling his house to help me complete the challenge, then his firm belief that this company is real may be genuine. All I would need to do then is to pay him back once I receive my money.

Briefly, HT shared that he was finally able to allocate some funds for me but that I would need to come up with the remainder to complete the challenge. He sent the allocated funds to my USDT wallet and showed me a screenshot of his transaction. So after seeing that screenshot, and on a last-minute whim, I made a request to cash out a portion of my IRA account to meet the requirement. I was able to submit my money to the trading platform on the last day of my deadline, which was on August 10. Customer service confirmed in a timely manner that they had received my payment.

After I made the request for withdrawal, customer service again quickly confirmed that they had received my request and advised me to wait patiently as the processing time would be 7-10 working days. On the day I received the confirmation from customer service, I noticed on the website the message "an upgrade is coming soon." Even though highly suspicious of that message, I then thought that, in this day and age, many websites are continually being upgraded for a better or more efficient user experience. So, I tried to bury that suspicion under the benefit of the doubt. However, my initial gut feeling turned into reality when a few days later, on Fri the 13th, the entire website went out of order. When I tried to log on to the website, the message "Network Abnormal. Unable to resolve this domain name" was displayed. I continued trying to log on for a few more days and eventually got the message: "This site can't be reached…(website domain) unexpectedly closed the connection. Try checking the connection."

Right after finding out the website was not working, I messaged HT and asked if he was able to access his account. He acted surprised and stated that he was very busy working the whole day and had not had a chance to log in yet. When I confronted him about the possibility of being scammed, he acted like he couldn't believe that could be happening. He reasoned that maybe there were a lot of people trying to withdraw their money because of the promotion, so the website was not able to handle the high volume and was temporarily down. I messaged him again a few days later, even as the website remained out of order. I asked him again if he had any issues with his previous withdrawal, and he reassured me that he never ran into any problems. Again, I brought up the extremely high probability of us having been scammed.

He said, once again, that he could not believe that might be happening because he had also already invested a lot of money in the platform. He said he chose to "believe" in this company because it was still in good standing and had served him and other close family and friends well before. He stated he would wait patiently and expect to see his money back in his account the following week. He claimed that the thought of losing all his money was unfathomable. But because we were unable to contact customer service, he agreed there was a chance I was correct in having my disturbing suspicion. At this point, he said he was in a very bad mood and would need to go away for some time to cool down and sort things out. He stated that he would now need to sort all his finances out and figure out what to do if my suspicion came true. He also dropped a hint to me that, unlike him, at least I still have some money in my account for necessities because he never really has that kind of money lying around outside of his investment accounts. His last words to me were, "please take good care of yourself and your family." Then he disappeared.

I couldn't believe that in such a short time, I had lost my entire life savings as a result of trusting someone who I had never met in person. After all of my money was gone, I woke up from the spell and realized how naïve I had been to give a stranger the benefit of the doubt when it came to financial advice. I was shocked at my poor judgment and blamed myself for my lack of discernment. I also blamed myself for trusting big corporations such as Facebook and Coinbase. I felt so stupid that I let my guard down and fell for something about which I should have known better. My entire life, I have always been cautious with money and aware of most types of scams out there. I knew how to save my hard-earned money and never risked losing much money in stock markets as I evenly distributed it through stocks, personal savings, 401k, and other retirement accounts. I never fell for any social security or job scams and watched out against Nigerian scams. I never fell for any sweepstakes, online shopping, gift cards, or Amazon scams. Nor have I ever fallen for emails or text messages with "urgent" notices regarding issues with my delivery, orders, or expired anti-virus subscriptions that I had never even subscribed to. I would never click on any links in my emails or text messages, and I would never respond to anyone I did not know or expected to hear from. I thought I was educated enough about the ongoing scams that I would be able to prevent myself from ever falling prey to one. Instead, I had walked myself right into the trap that my scammers had cleverly set up to lure me in by the use of psychological techniques and manipulation while posing to be a friend or potential partner for a long-term relationship.

I was utterly devastated when my fears turned into reality. I had just got scammed out of my entire life savings. My kids' college funds were gone, my emergency savings gone, my down-payment savings for a new house gone, and a portion of my retirement money were all gone. The realization made me feel like I was the dumbest person in the world. It made me lose trust in myself and my ability to make sound decisions. Not only did I lose faith in myself, but I also lost trust in society. I couldn't believe social media allowed these scammers to be lurking everywhere. I lost faith in the whole system. Because I was so embarrassed and ashamed, I dared not tell anyone what had happened. I figured people would only look down on me and ask, "how could you have fallen for that?"

For an entire week, I was in much despair and felt so helpless that I tried to sleep off all my feelings. I could hardly eat or drink anything in the first few weeks post-scam. I started to avoid everyone because I was so depressed and had no money to do anything. I stopped eating out the way I used to. I stopped seeing my friends even if we were to get together for just a walk. I just couldn't face anybody. I started making all kinds of excuses for why I couldn't go out or do a lot of things. I felt terrible for my children because I didn't have money to take them out or give them little treats to put a happy smile on their faces.

My entire world turned upside down as I no longer had the funds for their college or any for a rainy day. I had to start all over again from scratch. I knew at that point life would forever be different. As I was placed into survival mode from having lost everything all at once, I knew what I had to do. I knew I could not live the way I used to, even though it was never extravagant to begin with. I had to cut down on any spending that was not necessary and skimp out on just about everything. I stopped shopping for just about everything except the bare necessities. I quit cold turkey going to my favorite coffee shop for an entire year. Even though having my favorite drink every day made me feel happy, upbeat, full of energy and allowed me to focus better, I was willing or had to sacrifice my happiness to survive financially.

However, I felt I could not live under a shell forever and keep feeling sorry for myself. When I decided to tell a family member that I had lost all my money, he advised me to contact the police and the FBI. At first, I couldn't imagine anything these law enforcement could do if I reported the scam to them. I thought that in their minds, I was just another person who was very stupid to hand my money over to a criminal. I thought that they would blame me for authorizing all my transactions. But I decided to set aside my pride and started reporting to the authorities. Once I started sharing my story with the police and FBI, I found this gush of energy within myself to report to any organization I could to complain about my experience with the companies that allowed me to get scammed. I was so furious that I wanted someone to take down these companies involved in my scam. I wanted justice. So I decided to make phone calls to the Colorado Business Investigation Fraud Unit as well as the Colorado Secretary of State to report the fraudulent trading company. To my dismay, I discovered that no one in the state of Colorado was able to do anything with the scam company. Furthermore, I discovered that to apply for a business in Colorado, there was no process or regulation in place to screen out fake companies. So basically, anyone can just freely apply for a business license there. I was very disappointed that there is absolutely no regulation in place for businesses in Colorado to open and stay in business. Throughout the entire time I was using the fraudulent trading platform, which again seemed to be highly professional with a 24hr customer service, I thought I was investing in a legitimate company regulated by the state of Colorado and who Coinbase was doing legitimate business with. Since the state of Colorado could not do anything about the scam company, I tried to contact Coinbase. However, I never received any response from them. I felt that they could care less about my being scammed and just ignored my message. Later on, after listening to the numerous stories from members in our support group, my suspicion about Coinbase caring less for their consumers was confirmed. Many victims who had been scammed by the fraudulent companies reported the crime to Coinbase but had their personal accounts temporarily locked. Meanwhile, the fraudulent companies' accounts that were facilitating the scams that robbed the victims remained open. While some received responses from Coinbase stating there is nothing they can do, most victims continue to see their scammers' wallets grow in size while their own accounts are locked. I can't believe a company whose mission statement advertises that "everyone deserves access to financial services that can help empower them to create a better life for themselves and their families" would actually work with scam companies and, even worse, continue to work with them even after all the reporting they have received from numerous victims.

I was ashamed of myself for letting my guard down by thinking that a well-known US-registered company like Coinbase doing business with another US-registered company was nothing to worry about. I trusted not only my scammer, who I thought was a human being trying to help another human being, but the entire system where US-registered companies were supposed to be legitimate and conducting legal business. I blamed my downfall on being naïve in trusting well-known businesses that had promised to protect their consumers.

After contacting the Colorado Business Investigation Fraud Unit, the Colorado Secretary of State, and Coinbase, I also reported to BBB, FTC, and the California Department of Justice. The only response I received from them was they could not do anything about the fraudulent company, take any actions, or help me out.

After the scam, I instantly became skeptical of everyone and everything. Knowing that there were scammers out there posing to be a potential friend or business, I trusted no person or business moving forward. I wanted to fight and seek help to get my money back but now wisely reserved every right to be skeptical of any recovery companies advertising to help victims recover their scammed money.

However, in a desperate attempt to try to find my stolen money, I ended up trying to contact several "recovery" agencies. Now, being more alert than ever, I realized immediately that almost all of them were scam companies. Many "recovery" companies were asking for a huge upfront fee, usually in the tens of thousands. Even though one recovery company I found was listed under LinkedIn, I noticed many red flags after I contacted them. Their fee was over $10k and the contract they would have me sign had another victim's name on the form with different pricing. Many things did not add up, which convinced me that they were not a legitimate company. Some companies stated they could use software tools to trace where the money went and hack into the final wallet where the money ended up in. They would then take a considerable percentage of the recovered money for their work. If the hackers can do that, I thought to myself, they may as well just steal all your money instead of giving any back. Why would they even need to offer you help? While searching for recovery companies online, I was also shocked to find several forums where "victims" had shared how they successfully got their money back by using these "recovery companies" that they recommended. I looked at the emails and addresses of the recovery companies but found absolutely no information on them anywhere on the website. I was appalled to think that there were scammers out there posing to be victims to lure them in again to "help" the victims out. Although I eventually found a few legitimate recovery companies with reviews, it was hard to find evidence of actual recovery as everything was supposedly kept confidential to protect the victims. Since I never saw proof of victims ever getting any money back, I felt that it was best to steer away from any recovery companies.

Because I became skeptical of everything post-scam, I also couldn't trust any organizations that claim to be advocates for victims and offers to assist them post-scam. I came across GASO shortly after being scammed but did not want to enter another potential trap. However, after I followed GASO for several months and read articles of multiple PBS stories from victims themselves and realized how they were similar to mine, I started to think that maybe this is a real entity with good intentions. When I had initially discovered their website, it seemed like there was so little information on there, but then I noticed more articles being written even as I was following them. It was when I saw a list of scam companies which included my company, that I decided they were a legit organization. I finally decided to email them to thank and praise them for posting up the stories and scam company websites. To my surprise, I received an email response fairly quickly from the founder herself. After some exchanges, I was vetted into the US victim support group. This is how I came to join my current support group, which I have found extremely helpful because everyone had their own unique stories, and we learned a lot from each other. Most importantly, we knew we were not going through our pain and healing process alone. This support group is my biggest source of inspiration to write this book, and I am very grateful to finally find the courage to share our stories.

To all the people out there who look down on victims who have been scammed, thinking they are stupid and greedy, all I can say is it can happen to anyone. My being scammed has nothing to do with greed. I wasn't even looking to make an excessive profit or anything close to that but just trying to learn a system that could help me generate some positive income. I had no intention to exploit anyone to earn extra income but only thought of learning how I could better provide for my children and parents who could not support themselves. I am saddened and hurt to hear the perpetual false narratives from the media that portray victims as being greedy or ignorant enough to have given money to people they have just met. It is not as straightforward as the media portrays it since there were many processes that took place before the money ended up in the scammer's hands. On the contrary, scammers have mastered the use of sophisticated technology to wipe our banks clean, and there is just not enough exposure out there regarding the intricate and elaborate collaboration used to carry out their schemes. It hurts to hear the media blaming victims for falling prey because they are not wary or intelligent enough to see the red flags. All I can say is the PBS has victimized thousands of people in the US already in just the last few years and many more worldwide.

The whole scam was mind-blowing because I felt reverse psychology was used in my case to ultimately draw my interest into the fraudulent investment scheme. It was an elaborate ploy from beginning to end. I did not know that I would be fishing for a scammer when it is usually the other way around. In my case, I initiated the call. It began with the setup of a very attractive profile that was displayed on a very popular and commonly used platform for me to choose from. I had the freedom to choose who I wanted to talk to based on the descriptions under the profiles, so it was not like a stranger was randomly approaching me. The ploy involved the patience of the scammer taking the time to learn about me and vice versa. He employed normal human behavior on me and did not pressure me to do anything. The scammer allowed me to imagine what freedom may look like with every decision that I make for myself. He made me feel the beginning of freedom when I created my own username and password on my new account. When I brought up my concerns about paying taxes, he had a script pre-written for me: "you will not have to worry about paying taxes." He earned my trust by introducing me to a well-known and popular platform called Coinbase. He earned my trust by showing me how he had been investing alongside me. But all along, he had been playing me while he walked me into the ring of fire where his bosses were waiting for me. In the beginning, what seemed to be a very benign interaction led me to my total loss in the short time I engaged with that person.

It was a mind-altering experience for a person who had been overly cautious with money her entire life. From continually saving and planning on working until the recommended retirement age, to being persuaded to cut out a few more years under the assumption that she would be growing her money by learning a new form of investment, the decision to act under the persuasion that appeared to be reasonable took a turn for the worse. I started out being very content with where I was in life and with a good amount of savings. Then somehow, I was put under a spell that my scammer had gently unleashed, reminding me that he knows I am a smart person who can and will do the best thing for my family by investing in the form of a scheme that will give me financial freedom. Not to mention that Coinbase's mission also played a big role in that thought. The thought of not making the best decision for myself when there were opportunities to earn more and retire early made me feel guilty. Also recalling that just prior to meeting my scammer, a sibling had told me I was leaving money on the table when I had shared that I was putting some of my money under the mattress and some in the bank. Unfortunately, I let my guard down by opening up to the simple suggestion of placing my money in a platform where it could grow, and that was how curiosity ultimately killed the cat.

SC'S STORY

I will now share a story of a kind woman who lived a calm life until one day, the unthinkable happened. In just a few months, she came to lose a total of $800k. This is her heartbreaking story:

I want to forget this part of my life that brings back many painful memories. The scam has scarred me and made life really hard. I am still trying to find my way through the healing process. But today, I will open up the scar and find the strength to tap into those painful memories so that I can share my story. By doing so, I hope the innocent and kind people behind me will not fall for the same trap.

It all started when, one day in August 2021, my Century 21 real estate manager informed our group that she had a lead referral from Texas. She said the referral from Texas had received interest from a Facebook contact. This interested person is a Chinese woman looking to buy a house in the Beverly Hills area. Her buying price range is up to 4 million. My coworkers all got excited and wanted to contact her directly. However, the message we received from our manager stated that she doesn't speak English well and that her preferred form of communication is through WhatsApp. Since I was the only person who spoke Chinese in my group, I was designated to communicate with her. I did not know how to use WhatsApp, so my manager helped me download the app. The same night, I contacted the interested buyer. Her name is Li Siji.

From her profile picture, I thought the client was a beautiful and innocent young lady. When I contacted her, she shared many personal stories with me, so I thought she was a very sweet lady. She shared that she and her parents have a shoe business in China and also another one here in America. However, she claimed that due to the pandemic, the factory she had in America had to close. It was located in Seattle, WA.

Li Siji then revealed to me that she was divorced and had one baby boy. She wanted to try to make a better life for herself and her son by bringing him, as well as her parents, with her to enjoy a new life in America. She shared her plans for relocating to Los Angeles, CA. She was particularly interested in and hoping to settle in the Beverly Hills area.

I thought it was such a lovely story and perceived her as an innocent girl, who unfortunately, got divorced. Her story made me feel sympathy for her. Li Siji also said that her father has two brothers who have a close relationship and do business together. One of the brothers lives in the US, and the other in Hong Kong. She stated that her uncle in Hong Kong had success with investing and had taught her a lot about cryptocurrency. He was her mentor and guided her every step of the way to earning good money from cryptocurrency investment. She claimed that with the investment, she had made up for the loss in their shoe business, which did not do well during the pandemic.

I had a very good impression of this young lady who claimed to be heading out to Seattle with her uncle, who lives in the US, to clean up, close the factory, and try to get their life together. I asked her why she would want to buy a house instead of trying to rent first in the Beverly Hills area? Even though she mentioned that one of her uncles lives there, I suggested she only buy when she is familiar with the city and really likes living there. She replied pleasantly: "Wow, you are the only person who has said that to me. I really trust you because you would not just grab a buyer's money from a sale, but you really think about the buyer's benefit." She said that because she likes and trusts me, she wants to help me in return for being so kind and thoughtful. Her response of also wanting to help me get rich sounded legit at that time.

When I called her later to talk about the houses, she replied in a voice message stating she did not have time at the moment because she was doing online trading and would text me back when she was done. She contacted me after she finished her "trading" and informed me she had made another $8k in profit. I was surprised to hear that and asked, "Wow, how did you do it?" She replied, "I can teach you, but you cannot tell anybody, maybe just your husband and family." She stated that she did not want to teach anybody because she was not a teacher, so I thought that was very legit too. Of course, I realize now that her suggestion not to tell anybody should have been the first red flag.

She offered to teach me via WhatsApp. She mentioned using a cryptocurrency exchange platform called Coinbase. At that time, I had never heard of Coinbase. However, she informed me that it was a very legitimate company and that I could research them online as they are on the New York Stock Exchange. After checking myself, I was assured that I would be using a legitimate company. I thought to myself, I guess I can risk a $5k loss in a legitimate company, so I agreed to put in the money.

So, in September, I wired my first $5k from Bank of America to Coinbase. Afterward, I transferred the money from Coinbase to the company Li Siji has been doing her trading in called HLG. Once the money was in the HLG platform, she would teach me all the steps I needed to follow and show me how to make a little money. After I made a few hundred dollars, I got excited. I was wondering, while the current interest in the bank is zero point something percent at that time, how are some people able to get so rich? I thought that I was finally going to learn how through Li Siji.

I questioned her, "how can I get my money out if I want to withdraw the money?" She assured me that the money could go in and out freely. She even encouraged me to withdraw and make sure what I requested looked good in my bank account. Once I made the request to withdraw and saw the money back in my bank account, I felt relieved and thanked God I had met her because now I did not need to work so hard for every penny. I keep thinking, "so this is how rich people do it, right?" They invest their money to get more money?

As we continued to talk more about investment, she recommended I invest some money into the mempool. I asked her what that is, and she explained that for people to dig a coin, you will need a lot of equipment, space, and electricity. You are not digging but will be investing money into the process, and once they dig the coin, you can get a share of the money. The initial funds to do this will cost $100k. She talked about an offer that sounded so good that I felt like it was an opportunity too good to miss. She stated the returns for the first $100k is about $400 per day for only that one month. Afterward, that offer is no longer available.

I followed her suggestion, and on September 17, I put $100k into the mempool. Every day for the first month, my account reflected an increase of about $400 in interest, so I was getting very excited. On top of the interest, they also give you a sign-on bonus of a free coin, just like how you would get bonuses in Las Vegas. You can continue playing with your bonus through their online trading. By October, my initial deposit of $100k matured, and seeing the additional $400 daily was like, "wow." She said, by the end of the year, if you push to put in $500k, you will earn about $4k-$5k extra every day of income.

I told her I did not have $500k. She suggested finding somebody to borrow from. She continued to talk to me every day and night, walked me through more trading, and pushed me to put in a total of $500k to earn more income. She said by next year, she would be unsure of the situation but was confident that this year, I would be able to make extra money and that I already have the $100k in my account to begin with. Based on her calculations of my anticipated earnings, I would only need another $330k to make the total $500k to reach the $4k-$5k daily interest. Again, she said that the offer would only be for one month. Again, she tried to make it sound very attractive and too good to miss out on.

I was very hesitant but was also very excited. I thought to myself, "maybe if I could do this and find another $330k this year, I could surprise my husband with the extra money so he could retire early." So, I decided to take money out of my bank account, CD, and everything else I could think of. By the end of November, after some struggles and paying some early withdrawal penalties, I had gathered just enough money. I then again wired my money out of Bank of America to Coinbase and then to the fake HLG company.

As usual, she continued to talk to me every day. It felt nice to keep talking to her. In the meantime, I continued to look at homes for her. My husband and I went to Beverly Hills to check out the homes and even sent her videos of the tours we did. She would send back voice messages thanking us for making the trips. I was so naïve then, as I know now that everything was fake. Maybe it was an old man I had been talking to all along, but at that time, I just thought she was a sweet little girl who needed my help. I thought it was a mutual exchange where I help her adjust to life in America while she helps me obtain financial freedom. I thought I was the lucky one who was hit with the lucky charm.

After I deposited the $330k into the platform, my heart was pumping hard every day. I would check my account around the same times every day and can see my balance increase by $3k-$5k daily for the 30 days. The increasing balance seemed so attractive that I started to plan ahead and then also started to feel sorry for people who work so hard. I started thinking about all the people I could help once I learned this skill to make money. I was thinking I could help the homeless across the street and just started making beautiful plans. During this time, our relationship seemed to get closer and closer. Li Siji continued to talk about her business in Seattle. She stated that it would take them two months to close the factory but that later on, someone from Mexico would buy the business, so they would lose less. Then she would ask me about my shoe size so that she would bring some from her shoe factory to give to me as a present. We talked about a lot of different things here and there.

By December 19, my $500k had matured, so I planned to withdraw my money. However, I learned that I could not do so because customer service required me to first pay personal income tax for my profit earnings. I asked: "Why do I need to pay the tax? Taxes are my own problems." Customer service replied that it is a new law for the crypto business to charge tax before the withdrawal. So now I know why they had me do online trading every day so that my balance would be higher, which would give them a reason to require me to pay more tax. After making the extra earnings, which was about $470k, my total balance now shows $900k. They asserted that based on a 35% tax rate on the profit I made, I owed them $165k in tax. If I don't pay, then I cannot withdraw any money. However, if I pay in 48 hours, I can get my money back.

By December 24, I tried to figure out how to get more money to pay the tax so I could withdraw my money. I rushed to gather the funds and wired the same way into Coinbase and then to HLG. I then waited 24-48 hours for them to return my money, but that was when my nightmare began. Customer service did confirm that they had received my money. However, they informed me that I was on the waiting list to withdraw and that due to it being near the end of the year, many people are already attempting to withdraw as well. They said that since I am not a Diamond member, I do not have priority. However, if I want to become a member, I would need to pay another $60k, and they will not tackle a surcharge for Diamond members, which would have been another $30k-$40k.

So, I started thinking, "if I became a Diamond member, I would not need to pay a surcharge and would be able to withdraw my money quicker." While still contemplating that, I waited patiently and saw that my number was moving up very slowly, only by 2-3 people per day. I was #30,236 to take my money out. I asked why is my position moving up so slowly? Their reason was that more and more people were becoming Diamond members, and if I did not become a member, it might take about a half year to withdraw my money.

I really have no money at this point. When I tried talking to Li Siji, she informed me that she was with her uncle in Hong Kong because he had just gotten into a car accident and had lost consciousness. She had to extend our meeting date because she would not be back until February of next year. She also said that she could not help me at that time because China is very strict, so she would only be able to help me with a little money, about $25k. Since she was willing to put some money in to assist me, I thought then it must be true that she did want to help me. If she helps me, then I would need to pay an additional $35k to become a Diamond member. Again, I fell for another trap.

By the end of December, she claimed that she had mailed the money directly to the company because that was the only way she could help me, as she could not wire more in because Hong Kong is still regulated under China policy. At that time, I thought she still cared about me, so I had to figure out how to get another $35k in to try and meet the requirement.

Once I gathered and wired the money, I thought again that I could get my money back. However, I found out that that was not true when the next day, I received a message from customer service stating that the money she sent to the company did not go through because it was from Hong Kong. So now I had to figure out how to get the rest of the money. She apologized and said that she tried her best to help me. At this point, I just used my last bloody money to try to meet the requirement. Once I became a Diamond member, I had to wait 24-48 hours to get my money back. After 48 hours, nothing happened, so I messaged customer service again. They told me they would check to see what was going on.

When customer service got back to me, I was told that the money I had requested to withdraw was made to a different Coinbase address instead of the original one to which I had made my initial withdrawal request. Their exact quote is: "Your address is completely different from the withdrawal address you bind." They made up the excuse that Coinbase now changes accounts frequently, like every five days, so my account is now different than the original one I had signed up for and not in their initial contract for the withdrawal address. They stated Coinbase wanted to charge them $170k to correct the address. So even though they have my money in my account, they said they had to reverse that money out of my account to the original Coinbase address but will need to charge me the $170k to send it to the correct address. I called Coinbase to inquire about the charges, and they replied that they would never ask a customer for those charges and that I may have been scammed.

When I reached out to Li Siji, she started making excuses about my misunderstandings and sent instructions that I was to follow. She said she tried to teach me the correct way of doing things but that I had depended on her for everything and still didn't know what to do. She claimed that, without her, I had made some mistakes along the way. She showed me her true colors and just started blaming me for everything. She said because of my mistakes, I now had to pay the $170k. Otherwise, I would not be able to get my $800k back. She then accused me of being cheap and greedy. She completely gaslighted me and then disappeared for some time. Later on, she checked in on me and asked if I had ever deposited the $170k to get my money back and tried to recommend a loan company for me to borrow the $170k so that I could get all my money back. I told her I could not borrow any more money. She then replied she would not help me because she didn't even know me. That was the end of my story with her.

I am shocked, I am ashamed, and I don't know what to do. My bank is empty. I could not eat and lost 10 pounds in 2 weeks. My husband does not even know. When I was driving, it was very dangerous at that moment because I wanted to die. But I know that dying will not help. Thoughts were just running through my head, but I had to calm myself down. Things have already happened. I had to tell myself that I had lost just money. As long as I have my health, I can continue to work to get it back.

I finally had the courage to call the FBI and was told to report to IC3 and my local police. Whenever the authorities gave a suggestion or advice, I followed it. But I still don't have a case number, and no one contacted me until four months ago when I saw a police face to face who took down all my evidence. However, nothing else happened from there either. Desperate for help, I even called ABC's Denver 7 news after I saw a clip about a person who had lost 1.6 million from the PBS.[1] The person I contacted referred me to a local FBI agent by the name of Jason and also suggested that I contact Congress. So, I contacted Jason and did whatever he instructed me to do, but still, nothing happened. I then tried to reach out to Congress but was told they don't handle the type of crime I'm reporting, so I really have nowhere to go. As a last-ditch effort, I also tried using CNC to help me trace my wallet, but they did not have law enforcement involved. Since my money was all wired out from beginning to end, I also had zero chance of recovering my money from my banks.

I know my money is gone, but all I hope for now is that one day they will catch this monster. By telling my story, I am hoping someone can hear me. I wonder if I throw a little rock into the river, will anyone hear the water splash? I have a chunk of money thrown into the trash, but I want someone to listen to the sound I'm making. Even if I don't get anything back, I want to make some positive effort by sharing my story to make people aware.

Fast forward a few months after the scam, I got into a major car accident and ended up in the hospital with broken bones. So now, not only am I trying to cope with severe financial loss, but I am also trying to heal emotionally and physically. The impact of the scam had taken a tremendous toll on me that I wish would never happen to anyone.

CY'S STORY

CY is a member of our support group who mustered the courage to share his story with several journalists and became one of the first in our group to help create public awareness of the PBS. As with the initial media coverage from June 2022,[1] we will give this person the pseudonym "CY" to protect his identity. Furthermore, due to the severe traumatic memories it brings to relive his story, CY has given me permission to tell his story on his behalf.

CY is a 52-year-old man who lives in the San Francisco Bay Area. He has a wife and a teenage daughter who will soon enter college. Like most Bay Area professionals, he has a well-paying job and works hard to support his family. Because he is the more successful child in his family, he both supported his siblings and became his father's primary caregiver.

Everything seemed to be going well for CY until his father, who had been a long-time smoker, suffered from COPD (chronic obstructive pulmonary disease) and eventual heart failure. His father was sent to a convalescent home and lived there for the last four years of his life. During those four years, CY's stress levels increased due to the financial burden and responsibilities related to his father's medical treatment. In September 2021, his father's health declined drastically. If that wasn't bad enough, CY suffered the worst season of his life from a chain of events that happened from October through December 2021.

When his father became ill, CY was given a power of attorney for his father. On October 26, 2021, CY made the difficult decision to send his father to hospice. That action took a toll on his mental health. CY would go in and out of the hospital daily to care for his dying father, even on his own and on his wife's birthdays. On November 13, CY was on his way to visit his father at hospice, who at that time had been breathing through a loud ventilator. It would be the last night he would see his father. CY confessed that, during that evening, he had made a financial transaction that had drastically damaged his and his family's financial future. While in the hospital room, CY would play some old Cantonese songs while talking to his father and let him know that everything would be okay. He told his father that it is okay for him to move on if he is suffering. CY eventually dozed off at 1:30 a.m. but awoke at 1:45 a.m. The entire room was silent. His Bluetooth speaker had stopped playing the music, and his father was at peace. CY stated that this was the beginning of his nightmare.

During the month of October 2021, when CY was struggling to care for his ailing father, he randomly received a message on WhatsApp from a person identifying herself as "Jessica." She stated that she had reached out to him because his phone number was in her contacts, and she was wondering if he could be one of her old colleagues. Though he did not recall ever meeting this person, he replied that he does not remember her as an act of common courtesy. Somehow, Jessica was able to transform this "chance encounter" into an engaging conversation for CY. She was polite and warm, so CY enjoyed talking to her. She was engaging and talked to him about little things here and there. She would then share pictures of the food she was eating, and the small talk would eventually push CY to open up about his current struggles with being able to support his family and ailing father.

By December 3, after several months of conversing with Jessica on WhatsApp, CY was in financial ruin, and his world was shattered. This "Jessica," who he thought would be a friend, had turned out to be the greatest deception of his life. After tricking him into investing money through trading on the Meta Trader app, he would ultimately lose $1.2 million.

The scam began as a seemingly innocent conversation with Jessica randomly sharing with CY how much "profit" she had been making through trading on Meta Trader. Since he was already persuaded to like and trust Jessica, CY moved the conversation along by asking her how she did so well and wondered how she had learned these investment skills. Jessica shared that she had learned from her "uncle," who lives in the same area of Hong Kong where his parents were from. She said that he would give her insider gold trading tips. At that time, CY was not suspicious of Meta Trader since it was a well-known trading platform, and their app was available for download from the Apple App Store.

At first, CY wondered why Jessica wanted to share insider trading secrets with him. She responded by revealing that she also has a grandfather in the hospital, so she understood what CY was going through and that she did not want him to have to work so hard. She suggested that, since she could get insider information from her uncle, he should learn the secrets so that he could make some good profits and use that money to help his family. CY was unsure about getting into trading, but Jessica suggested that he should listen to her if he wanted to make some money to help his family. He shared that he is not greedy and that if he were to lose all his money, he would kill himself.

Eventually, after long conversations and more persuasive stories, including how she had made $5 million out of her initial $5 million investment, CY agreed to try her suggestion. At that time, he contemplated how he could help other people if he could earn the additional investment income. He also thought about how nice it would be for his wife to work less since she had been working hard her entire life and how he may also be able to afford to send his daughter to college. On October 17, per Jessica's instruction, he downloaded the Meta Trader 5 app.

Jessica patiently instructed CY to download the trading platform connected to Meta Trader and showed him how to trade there. To start, she had him do a simulated trading without any money so that he could test the platform and get comfortable using it. She would kindly walk him through, step-by-step, how to do the trades. In the beginning, he had lost and gained some money through the simulated trade. After a few more trades, the simulation had him gain more money.

On October 20, Jessica asked CY to deposit a minimum of $10k so that he would be able to maximize his profits and use the extra income to help his family. However, CY was hesitant to invest $10k because he was already in a financial bind. He requested that Jessica put in $5k, and he would put in the other $5k. Then, once he made the profit, he would pay her back. Jessica refused to comply with that request and explained that he would not need to make his own money if she gave him money. CY responded by stating he wanted to be comfortable with the process and assured her that he would return the borrowed money, not keep it. Jessica earned his trust by agreeing that it is normal to be careful the first time you try an investment.

After some conversations back and forth, Jessica used reverse psychology on CY by telling him, "Don't do it if you are worried," and remarked that "men should not behave like this" because he did not want to deposit the entire $10k. Her statements got CY to eventually agree to put in his first $10k. He attempted to wire $10k from his bank to Coinbase but transferred the money to Crypto.com instead due to technical issues with Coinbase. The money in CY's Crypto.com account was then converted to USDT, in compliance with Jessica's instructions. Once the USDT was transferred to Meta Trader, he was led to believe that he would use the platform to buy gold futures. Even though CY saw his money grow as he followed Jessica's instructions, he was still nervous about the risk of trading his money. However, he continued trading with the belief that he would be risking his money in service of helping with his father's medical expenses and a chance to provide a better future for his family. He felt confident that the platform he was using was real, so he agreed a week later to deposit more money and continued to watch it grow.

Meanwhile, in between his trades, CY would continue to confide in Jessica about the stress he anticipated after meeting the doctors to determine his father's fate. He even shared how he had to do the same for his mother eight years prior. Although Jessica pretended to have sympathy, she told him to accept the things that had already happened. CY further confided in her how he felt his purpose in life was to take care of his siblings, parents, and family since he believed he was born by accident. Jessica used that opportunity to say she wanted to help him because he was so filial.

CY felt nervous throughout the investment process since he had never dealt with so much money. But Jessica would manipulate him by asking if he doubted her when she had repeatedly reassured him that she had been making a lot of money with her uncle's insider information. As they continued trading, CY was encouraged by watching his balances grow every day. Per her continual suggestions, he continued to deposit more money.

Before CY initially agreed to try out the investment, he told her that he would only do it as long as it was safe. Since Jessica had him download Meta Trader directly from the Apple App Store, he was not worried because he assumed it was a legitimate trading platform after seeing that it had a high rating of 4.7 stars. But little did he, or anyone who has fallen into the scammer's trap, know that the platforms they were using were only a convincing replica of the real brokerages. The transactions and profits were all controlled and manipulated by other scammers working behind the scenes, with the host scammer responsible for walking the victims into the trap. Meta Trader both works with real brokerages and offers licenses for its software which scammers are able to use to manipulate market prices and simulate just about everything, including the profits, losses, and balances.[2,3]

As CY felt more comfortable doing the trading, he was persuaded by Jessica to add more funds. After seeing his profits continuing to increase, Jessica would talk about the "big market" coming and the benefits that he would receive if he took advantage of the limited-time opportunity before it was too late. CY had already informed Jessica he did not have more money to invest.

As CY continued to spend most of his days in the hospital attending to his father, Jessica played with his emotions and asked if he missed her even though he was busy worrying about his father and how he would be able to pay the mounting bills. She then pretended to say that she was worried about him and acknowledged the difficult time he was going through. She would say she was serious about him and reminded him not to forget to eat. She gave him the feeling that he would always have her for emotional support.

However, amid her "sympathy" and "worries" for him, she still managed to sell him some "urgent" financial advice. On November 4, she advised CY to sell his stocks. She would remind him again on November 5 of the urgency, to which CY replied that he should be mourning and not talking about money. Jessica persuaded him that his father would have wanted him to do better financially, so it is not something that he should worry about.

CY was persuaded that he did not want to miss out on the "big market" opportunity. By that evening, CY had reached $300k principal. Jessica urged him to put in a total of $500k to be able to earn the extra profits. Since he did not have enough cash to deposit, Jessica pretended to loan him some money, about $60k. To reciprocate, he promised to look for the rest of the funds to reach the $500k goal.

After persistent nudging, she pushed him to liquidate his stocks and other assets as his father's condition worsened. If investing $500k was not enough, Jessica pushed him even harder to put in a total of $1 million. She advised that he borrows money from family and friends though he replied that he did not want to do that. To fund his trading platform account, he continued to sell more assets and withdrew $200k from the equity on his home. Eventually, he was able to gather $440k of his own money by November 14. That day, CY's father passed away. He felt lost and hopeless. He turned to Jessica to let her know she was now his only hope. Of course, Jessica again took his despair and used that as her opportunity to encourage him to depend on her for emotional support.

Jessica continued to guide CY with transactions on the trading platform. On November 18, the "big market" day had finally arrived, and CY could not believe that his $440k investment had already grown to $2.2 million. However, during a critical trade, Meta Trader showed his balance suddenly dropping to a negative $480k. CY thought there must be something wrong with the app and that maybe it had crashed. Jessica explained that if his principal is not enough, his trade cannot bring him to a profit. But she confidently reassured him that she could bring him back. He felt he had no choice but to agree with her since all his money was gone.

Her instruction to him was to increase his funds. Desperate to bring back his money, CY agreed to allocate more funds. He believed that since he could gain $1.7 million in just two weeks, he should be able to do this again, and trusted that her insider information was accurate. Therefore, he continued to liquidate any remaining assets. Jessica continued to suggest that he borrow money from his family and friends. CY eventually managed to borrow $100k from a childhood friend. Along with all the assets he liquidated, he was able to bring in an additional $600k. On top of the original $440k he had invested, CY had now put in a total of $1.2 million of his own funds.

With the $600k he had deposited, CY continued to trade to try to bring back all his money. On December 2, his balance reflected $1.1 million. Seeing that his initial loss of $440k has now been offset, CY felt relieved. Jessica encouraged him to trade until he reached $1.8 million, and once he reached that amount, she would teach him how to withdraw his funds. To CY's disbelief, his account showed a negative balance the next day. When he desperately pleaded for help from Jessica that day, she turned the cold shoulder and said she could not help him. Instead, she advised that he contact the police.

CY could not believe that he was butchered twice! He had lost his first batch of money on November 23 and the rest on December 3. Devastated and traumatized by everything that had happened, CY checked himself into the UCSF hospital. It was the day after his daughter's 15th birthday. He entered the psychiatric ward on December 4 under suicide watch. He blamed himself for everything. He blamed himself for losing all his and his family's hard-earned money, as well as his daughter's tuition for college. He blamed himself for increasing his wife's working hours when he sought to do the opposite. He thought about running his car into a barrier and letting God decide if he would live or die.

CY suffered severe depression and struggled every day with guilt and blame. For many months, CY kept losing hope and wanted to quit. He had suicidal ideation on many occasions. He vented that he was alone for three months before he found GASO and felt so grateful to have finally joined in. Although he wished he had discovered GASO sooner because he was going through the entire post-scam experience alone, he was glad to find the support. However, despite the support everyone has tried to provide him, CY still feels much pain and hurt as I write his story today. The month of December marks the first anniversary in which he ultimately lost all his money, and he admits the trauma still paralyzes him.

On a more positive note, CY is one of three PBS victims we know of who will regain a portion of his stolen money.[4,5] He contacted all the law enforcement channels he could think of and eventually reached the REACT team, who was able to act on his case right away. Through extensive investigation, the REACT team was able to freeze and seize a portion of his stolen money which was stored in USDT in a random and unknown scammer's wallet at Binance. It is exceedingly rare for victims to get their money back since most investigations lead to a dead end. The money is typically laundered immediately after it has been transferred to the wallet. CY was fortunate to be getting back about $113k out of the $1.2 million he had lost.

Although it is rare to hear of any money being recovered, there may be hope as American law enforcement teams are continually learning more about this super scam. With more information provided promptly by the PBS victims to all the relevant agencies, especially those whose mission is to "protect consumers" and US citizens from cyber scams and fraud, more public awareness alerts will be issued. Although it may be too late for most victims who have lost their money in 2021-22, with time and experience, it may be possible for the authorities to catch up to the criminals by disrupting the ease at which they have exploited loopholes in the cryptocurrency market.

A kind GASO volunteer created a GoFundMe page for CY. Post-scam, he had to deal with several emergencies, including a gas and water leak, which further added to his financial strain. If you can help out in any way, CY would greatly appreciate your support. You can donate at this link: https://gofund.me/fad84aff.

| AM'S STORY

I would like to share a heart-rending blog from another member of the GASO support group, AM. Through AM's writing, we can see one of the many ways victims of the PBS have been emotionally impacted. Her saga, and especially her graceful attitude, has greatly inspired me. Despite having lost her entire life savings and borrowed money and coping with her pain and emotions as described in her blog, she was able to encourage herself to "never give up, no matter what" and urged every other PBS victim to do the same. As I am writing today, eight months after AM wrote her blog, she declares that life can never knock down those who refuse to fall and continues to encourage me and others to fight on and never give up hope. She vouches, "I will fly again and fly higher this time!"

AM's story begins with a conversation on LinkedIn, a trusted platform for business networking. Because she was victimized through this platform, AM would like to dispel the myth that the PBS only happens as the result of a romantic relationship.

However, she admits that, although the scammer had initially tried and failed his romantic attempts with her through LinkedIn, in the end, he ultimately succeeded in his goal of robbing her of all her money. She did not think she would have ever gotten scammed, at least not through LinkedIn. Her total loss was $288k.

At the time the scam started, AM was a 42-year-old manager in a Florida benefits department. She was contacted by a person through LinkedIn who claims on his profile to be a manager at a fitness company in Los Angeles. The request to connect seemed like an innocent one. He began the conversation by asking if she was on LinkedIn for professional networking or looking for a job. At the time she was approached, AM was thinking about building her dream business.

AM informed me that she is the type of person who does not trust anybody and believes she has to do everything herself. She said she would only earn trust once she sees the proof. Furthermore, she says that throughout her entire life, she had worked very hard for every dollar and knew how to save every dollar she earned. So, she would always proceed with caution if anyone suggested how she should use her money.

Although AM is generally untrusting of people, she somehow let her guard down with the new person she connected with on LinkedIn. The man, who was dressed in a professional suit in his profile, was TL. He initially contacted her in English, but when he found out she could also speak Chinese, he shared that he also speaks Chinese, so they switched their conversations from English to Chinese. Their conversations went smoothly in their native language. He initially tried to start talking romantically with AM, but she let him know right away that she was not interested in pursuing a romantic relationship since she was already in a committed relationship. Unable to immediately come up with an engaging response or clever comeback, TL disappeared. However, he returned a few days later and asked if they could just be friends.

Once AM agreed, TL switched gears and further engaged her through different topics. She soon revealed to TL her dream of starting her own business. AM's story is truly a delicate one, as her reason for looking for a new job was prompted by her health issues. She shared with TL that she was hoping to find a new job that would be less physically demanding. She shared how she was physically struggling daily with her debilitating nerve pain, which resulted from an accident many years ago, and which she has endured most of her adult life. The injuries she suffered from the accident took a significant toll on her health and finances. Due to the chronic nerve pain that flares up frequently, she was interested in pursuing a career that would not put further strain on her health and feet.

It was TL's sympathy that made her feel like he understood her pain. He displayed interest in finding ways to help her. She thought that he cared for her when he tried to come up with suggestions on how she could work or make money without enduring more physical pain. He would also check in with her daily and ask how her pain level was each time. He would make sure she ate breakfast and took good care of herself.

After conversing for a little while, TL asked AM to move their conversation from LinkedIn to WhatsApp since he stated he does not use LinkedIn often. AM agreed since that request didn't seem to be anything out of the ordinary. However, due to some "challenge" on WhatsApp, TL asked to switch their conversation to LINE. Again, AM did not make anything out of that request either since she and her friends were already using LINE.

Over time, AM felt more comfortable talking to TL and started to trust him. Once he earned her trust, TL made the suggestion of investing in cryptocurrency on the side as a backup for her income in case there are days when she is unable to work due to her pain. He then showed her how he had been profiting from investments and suggested she try it herself. That suggestion did not seem unreasonable or to trigger any red flags at the time, and she was curious how cryptocurrency investment would work as a side investment. However, like many PBS victims, she was initially skeptical about getting into cryptocurrency investments. TL minimized her fear and made her feel comfortable by suggesting that she only try the investment with a little bit of money, only $400 to start.

Once she felt convinced that TL was genuinely trying to help her, she opened up to his advice. TL recommended using Crypto.com for exchanging her currency. Since AM was aware that Crypto.com was a legitimate platform, she agreed to put in her initial $400 on December 14, 2021. That money would be converted to USDT and then transferred to the trading platform TL recommended. Before downloading the app for the trading platform, AM did her due diligence by calling her own phone company to verify if the app she would be downloading on her iPhone was safe and legitimate. Apple support confirmed that there was no harmful code or virus in the app and assured her that it was safe to download it on her phone. Once the company website was verified in good standing, AM felt comfortable using the trading platform. There, TL would teach her how to make the trade. She was pleasantly surprised to see her balance grow and note how relatively easy it was to make money through cryptocurrency investment.

But she was still skeptical about being able to see her money back. Once TL showed her how to withdraw her money and send money back to her bank account after making the request herself, she started trusting TL more. She was happy to see that her money from the trading platform was successfully sent back to Crypto.com, then from there back to her original bank account. TL said that teaching her how to withdraw her money and making the extra profit was her Christmas present from him. Once the withdrawal process was complete, she received a total of $1k back in her bank. This amount reflects the $600 profit on top of her initial $400 investment. After doing some more trading and earning profits, AM did not inform TL that she had secretly attempted to withdraw more money to make sure the system worked under her own initiation. To her surprise, she was able to receive her money back smoothly from the second withdrawal request. AM claimed that, after having worked nonstop her entire life, she was beginning to think that God had sent someone her way to help make her life easier.

To make a long story short, AM would eventually take out all $110k of her savings and even leverage her perfect credit score to secure some bank loans, per TL's suggestions. Within two months, she had made a total of nine transactions. Per TL's advice, she had also borrowed a total of $150k, including a high-interest loan. Some of the money she borrowed was from friends who were hoping to see her open up a new café business which she had long been dreaming of.

Within a two-month period, when AM's balance reflected $650k, she decided it was time to withdraw. However, she was informed that there would be a delay in the withdrawal process due to many people trying to withdraw at the same time. Customer service informed her that she would have to pay extra to get in front of the line for a withdrawal request. A few days later, when trying to log onto her account, she noticed a message on the website stating it was temporarily out of service for maintenance. Since she was not able to log on, she tried to contact TL. But he never responded and seemed to have disappeared. When she tried to log on again the day after, she received a message on the website, "This website may be impersonating you to steal personal or financial information. You should close this page."

AM realized, in the end, that the person she had been talking to was not who he claimed to be. She was devastated to realize that when all her money disappeared, TL had also disappeared.

Because AM had worked so hard for her money and had hopeful ambitions in her career, the scam was truly a painful experience. She, like many other victims, said that her world had turned upside down. She was hurt to know that someone on LinkedIn would purposely intend to defraud her by befriending her. She could not believe she was deceived by a fake persona who claimed to work for a legitimate company. As she and many other victims have discovered post-scam, there were many fraudsters hiding behind LinkedIn profiles pretending to work for legitimate companies. She could not believe that other victims had also been scammed through LinkedIn and lost their entire life savings and more. Some victims have reported losing their homes and cars. As a result of letting their guard down, many people who have been victimized through the LinkedIn platform have ultimately blamed themselves for their loss.

Since AM could not pay the high-interest loans back, she had no choice but to file for bankruptcy. This would be the second time she would have to file for bankruptcy. In her blog below, AM described how she came about declaring her first one. While still looking for a new job, AM would have to reveal and declare to her employer that she had filed for bankruptcy due to being a victim of the scam. Her perfect credit score was completely ruined. She had to start her life over. Below are the two blogs she wrote months after the scam to share how she coped.

Will I Every Fly Again?

April 12, 2022

I decided to blog today because I seriously feel helpless, hopeless, and bitter with my life. I came to the United States of America about 23 years ago, right after I finished high school in a third-world country in Asia. It was my dream to come to America and pursue my dream to be a useful person in society and contribute to this world. It was so hard in the beginning because I only spoke a little English. I worked full time and went to school full time. College was really hard for me because when I wanted to learn something, I had to understand that in Chinese first. Then, I would translate it into my native language, then finally translate it into English and vice versa when I wanted to express myself. It was so hard for me. In 2005, I got into a car accident and suffered severe injuries. I did not die, but I was in a wheelchair for a year. I eventually managed to walk again with a cane, but I do not need it to walk anymore. I cannot run anymore either. I had brain damage and lost a lot of my memories as well. I had to file for bankruptcy due to the quarter million dollars' worth of medical bills. My personality changed a bit, and I think I became happier.

I told myself I would not give up. I will stand up again. I went back to school to get my degree. I worked two full-time jobs and went to school part-time, and I finally got my bachelor's degree. I had brain and nerve damage, so I lived in pain almost every day. After years of living in a tiny efficiency apartment, I saved up to buy my first house in 2019. I worked hard. I saved money and I took care of those that I love. I do not like to complain because I believe the only way to overcome a challenge is to put in the effort. I consider myself a strong woman, but once in a while, I need a shoulder to cry on as well. I am working full-time now. There are days I am in pain and shaking but have to continue working. I live with chronic pain every day. On the days when the pain is severe, I feel tortured, but nobody understands.

People only see how much I get paid. I was very unhappy, but one day in December 2021, someone reached out to me via LinkedIn. He started the conversation as you would on a dating app. I told him I was not interested because LinkedIn is a professional networking site, and he disappeared for a few days. He messaged me again. This time he tried to make a connection by discussing how we are of the same ethnicity and have similar interests. As we talked more, he made me think he was someone I could talk to as a friend, someone who understood me, and wanted me to have a good life despite my physical limitations. We moved our chat to WhatsApp, then to LINE. He convinced me to start investing in cryptocurrency. I usually do not trust people, but he has a way of making me trust him. With his instructions, he took me to a fake platform to trade cryptocurrency. I see that I am making money, and he said I should withdraw $1k to my bank as his Christmas present to me. I did that and received $1k in my bank. I thought, finally, God had sent someone to my life to make it easier. I was also happier during that period since I felt like I had someone to talk to. One day without him knowing, I tried to withdraw some money, and it worked as well. I began to trust him more.

As time went by, he convinced me to invest not only all my money but also take out some loans to make more profits. My goal was to have enough money so that I could have a small business and my life would be a little easier. When I saw my account balance on the fake platform reached over a half-million, I decided to take out the money so that I could pay back the loans and start planning for the business. However, that was when I found out things were not the way I thought. I could not withdraw the money. Customer service requested me to put in more money in order to withdraw. However, I have no more money. I even borrowed some money from a couple of close friends. I know that I was scammed.

I checked online and realized that I fell for the so-called pig butchering scam. I reported to many government law enforcement authorities. I know that my money is gone no matter what. He disappeared completely as well. I feel hopeless and keep telling myself to stay strong. I realized I had to file for bankruptcy because there is no way that I could pay back the loans that I had taken out. I am so tired and ready to leave this world, but I cannot do so because I still owe a few of my friends money. I should, and I need to pay them back. They helped me, and I cannot just leave like that. I told myself to be strong and overcome this challenge as well. I am so very tired though. Seventeen years ago, I filed for bankruptcy and tried so hard to get to where I was. Now, I have to do it all over again. I wish that I could donate my life to someone who needs it. I do not see the reason I keep fighting. Every time I stand up, I get knocked down again. I live in physical and mental pain every second. I feel like a bird with a broken wing and a wounded heart. Will I ever fly again?! 💀

EVERY SINGLE BREATH I TAKE HURTS. THIS IS THE PUREST OF PAIN!

AM I TOO GREEDY TO ASK FOR AN EASIER LIFE AFTER ALL I'VE BEEN THROUGH? GOD SAVE ME, PLEASE!

Painful Journey of Trying to Fly again~

April 15, 2022

After being scammed, I go to bed every night and wake up every morning with tears in my eyes. I would not say I'm crying because I know I have to keep fighting, no matter how I feel physically and mentally. It hurts, but I am trying my best to stay strong and continue the journey. Whether I walk or crawl, I know I have to continue. There are days I feel a little better than others. Just as usual, I have to stand back up by myself. I am scared, lost, and lonely. This time I am glad that I joined the support group at GASO. The victims in this group try to support each other. Starting over in my 40's with nothing but physical limitations is very scary.

December 30, 2022

"We are all only guests on this Earth. We came empty handed, and we will leave empty handed. Why not enjoy the journey?"

| PSYCHOLOGICAL MANIPULATION

"We've realized that everybody is a potential victim. Because we're all human, we're all vulnerable to the emotional manipulation and patient grooming prevalent in scams."

-Grace Yuen, Global Anti-Scam Organization media spokeswoman

As you can see from these stories just told, even though the outcomes were the same for all the PBS victims, with their life savings and trust in humanity abruptly hijacked, each victim experienced a unique version of the PBS. This demonstrates how sophisticated the PBS can be. The tactic each perpetrator uses to carry out each crime can vary greatly. Furthermore, although the PBS has been known as more of a romance investment scheme whose targets were usually the more lonely and vulnerable populations such as the elderly, single, or widowed, the crime has become more elaborate and advanced over time, so that just about anyone is susceptible to becoming a target. Again, as demonstrated in the few stories told in this book, even those who are married or in committed relationships can fall victim. It cannot be emphasized enough that there is no "typical" profile for a PBS victim.

One thing to never underestimate is how successful the scammers have been at what they do. These criminals defraud for a living and focus day in and day out on developing creative, new ways to trick you. The criminals in the cyber scam industry are always trying to stay ahead of you and will use every new technology to their benefit. They will continually refine their techniques and adjust to society as it changes and advances. It is a full-time job, and in the name of greed, they do not care who they defraud.

The most crucial factor in their success is understanding the universal mechanics of persuasion and emotional vulnerability. Criminal masterminds have studied human psychology extensively and love to exploit vulnerabilities. They will devote their time to thoroughly study and analyze innate human behavior. The PBS is often successfully carried out through extremely advanced social engineering. Criminals will make the "kill" by hacking the human subconscious to slowly take control of their targets over time by subtly instilling messages in the victims and leading them to believe that what they have been hearing is true. For example, all PBS scammers, regardless of where you have met them or what relationship you might find with them, will use constant flattery to manipulate your emotions by repeatedly saying that you are intelligent, attractive, funny, and especially responsible until they have sufficiently hijacked your thoughts. This is when the subtle programming of your mind begins. Over many days of this type of persistent messaging, the criminals will become the driving force behind your thoughts and actions.

The masterminds behind these scams have developed meticulously written scripts and training manuals that are tailored to every possible personality type, which "new recruits" are coerced to follow. There is a script[1] for everyone, depending on age, gender, profession, socioeconomic background, etc. They carefully study each target and learn as much about them as possible, including each person's unique strengths and weaknesses. As they continue to carefully study human behavior across all cultures, genders, age groups, professions, and so forth, the manuals are being updated, and human trafficking victims are exploited to perpetrate the crimes concocted in the name of the crime syndicate masterminds' greed.

The PBS syndicates have an elaborate criminal network with head offices and branch locations, most of which are located throughout Southeast Asia. They have specialized teams working for them, including IT, telecom, money laundering, and sales departments.[2] They will entice their workers or captives with commissions for the successful "slaughters." They will send their recruits to "classes" that teach them finance terminology. Recruits will also learn how to use tools such as Google Translate so that they are better able to communicate with their targets. Using free American technology to translate scripts written in Chinese directly into English and other languages, they are able to defraud English and other non-Chinese speaking targets.

In the beginning, the forced recruits (captives) are trained to cleverly use techniques of psychological manipulation and persuasion to ultimately enhance the target's compliance with agreeing to try out the investment that they have been recommended. Recruits are guided through each step with their training manuals. These manuals are flexible since their bosses can switch gears and update them based on their interactions with the targets. When a recruit is stuck at any point with how to proceed with their prey, more experienced recruits will switch shifts with them to continue the scam process. If still unsuccessful in fulfilling the agenda, their supervisor would step in to carry out and complete the job.

The first step of the PBS requires that the lower-level agent scour social media and networking sites to seek potential targets (analogous to generating sales leads). Their job is to look presentable and likable with an impressive profile. Once they lure and befriend their target, their next goal is establishing trust. Meanwhile, the recruits will be forced to spend days and nights (often under the threat of torture) inventing ways to defraud each unique individual that they have met online. To hook the attention of their targets, they will come up with stories of how they and their targets have something in common, such as having lived in the same city during their childhood, attended the same college, or shared similar interests. The scammers will then present themselves as hardworking, trustworthy, and family-oriented. They will make sure to mention their aunts, uncles, or parents and then pretend to care for the target and their family. If the target has any physical, mental, or family issues, they will pretend to be empathetic. They will pretend to show that they care and foster trust by stressing the important things in the target's life that are valued the most, such as their family and health. Although they will come up with excuses as to why they can never meet in person, they will make sure to check in daily to see how their target, children, parents, and even their pet, if they have one, are doing.

While they pretend to be a good listener and care about the target and their family, the scammer's plan is to slowly learn small details about the target to understand their pain points and vulnerability to tailor the script later on. The more they learn, the more they will use this to make the target feel valued. Slowly, after the target has revealed enough personal information, the scammer will give the target reasons to make them feel smart and responsible. This will increase the probability of compliance by encouraging them to use their intelligence to make the best financial decisions for their family. Once the scammer earns the target's complete trust, the target's thinking has been influenced enough for them to let their guard down and give their "friend" the benefit of the doubt. At this point, the scammer will use the target's trust to their advantage by manipulating the target's ways of thinking and influencing their decision-making. For example, they will use the prospect of a better future and early retirement to get the target into a dreamlike, almost hypnotic state and provoke emotions of excitement.

With enough persistence and calculated use of persuasion techniques, they eventually succeed in convincing the target that putting their money into investment makes practical sense for a brighter future so they will be able to support their family better. The criminals will even continue to earn the target's trust through their suggestions of involving family members in their new venture of building collective wealth. These investments are always framed as a "business partnership" to cause disassociation in the target and further erode any sense of independent agency. By walking the target through the trading platform and showing them how to make withdrawals, they further continue to earn their target's trust as the target establishes a stronger feeling of dependency. Of course, while watching their "earnings" grow on the fake trading platform, the money is already long gone. Contrary to how the media usually portrays it, the victim did not simply hand over the money to the scammer. The victim was led to believe that the money in the trading platform was safely stored under their own name. However, the wicked reality is that those funds were most likely immediately laundered away by multiple scammers. Where did the money go? Of course, to fund operations. But perhaps also to North Korea or to buy drugs for the cartel's boss. With the anonymity of the blockchain and the current state of chaos and lawlessness in many Southeast Asian countries, the end destination of the stolen funds is difficult to ascertain.

The more they practice, the more expert at their craft they become over time. For example, in our society, we have been told from a very young age that we should always treat others how we want to be treated. This is one of the human tendencies that scammers have employed to manipulate the target's behavior. They always employ the principle of reciprocity[3] (first identified by the social psychologist Robert Cialdini) to make their targets feel that, since they are being helped, they should do something in return. Scammers use this well-known principle of persuasion to manipulate the victim into thinking that their "new friend" is genuinely helpful. Then they feel indebted to do something in return to show their gratitude. A popular use of the principle of reciprocity is when the scammer provides a "generous" wire transfer deposit into the victim's simulated account (a large sum, such as $25k) to prove that they are helping the victim reach new heights. They will say this is shared money, so it is no big deal, and they trust the victim. Thus, the victim feels indebted and has an increased sense of trust in the scammer since the deposit looks legitimate.

Scammers will ask questions to gather information and then do anything they can to try to "push your buttons." If you have kids, they will persuade you to invest so that you can use the profit to pay for their college tuition. If you have a spouse, they will tempt you to invest so that your earnings will reduce their need to work long hours. If you have elderly parents, they will entice you to invest to make their life easier. If none of those apply, they will try to convince you to wisely invest your money so that you can shower yourself with a nice vacation, a new car, or even a house. They will convince you that you deserve to treat yourself after all those years of hard work and encourage you to retire early because you deserve that break. They will make it all about you and sell these dreams to create disassociation with our normal sense of the financial future, disrupting the normal anchoring[4] to prices in the real-world economy. They will then use these dreams to jack up quotas for the minimum requested to "trade." Since these goals are incredibly expensive, it becomes more normal to deposit ever-increasing amounts of money to work up to a $500k target to pay for your children's college tuition, early retirement, property, or whatever the dream may be.

Although scammers generally target people who are good-natured and compassionate since people with these traits tend to be easier to manipulate, they have successfully targeted people on the opposite spectrum. They will use persuasion techniques to manipulate even the most careful and skeptical people.

Unfortunately, many people in our support group who have been victimized are the good-natured and caring type. We believe that kind people tend to project their good-naturedness onto others. Kind people not only believe in the good of humanity but are also more likely to sacrifice for others. Because people with these traits do not automatically recognize that not everyone out there also has good intentions, scammers cynically exploit this vulnerability. Healthcare professionals who are also usually caring and nurturing in nature are easy targets since they are generally so busy saving lives that they do not have reason to question the malicious intentions of other people who serendipitously befriend them.

Regardless of what types of people the media portrays as easy targets, such as the lonely, elderly, and vulnerable, the truth is that people from all walks of life have become victims of the PBS. The victims' age range can also vary greatly, from young adults to retirees. Although the PBS originated in Southeast Asia and was initially crafted to target Chinese and other Asians, scammers have successfully used their techniques to victimize people of all different races, socioeconomic backgrounds, and geographic regions. Even highly educated and influential people, including politicians, lawyers, doctors, nurses, business executives, engineers, accountants, realtors, bankers, financial analysts, computer programmers, police, athletes, actors, as well as cybersecurity employees, have all fallen victim to the PBS. People who are financially literate and academically accomplished are usually the ones who have established substantial savings and can, therefore, be enticing targets. Unfortunately, many are unprepared for the social engineering tactics applied to "chance encounters" and custom scripts specially tailored to every personality type and life situation.

The PBS criminals will continue to invent new ways to befriend anyone for the sole purpose of stealing their money. For every interaction that they have with new victims, they will continue to learn the latest trends, lifestyles, foods, popular hangouts, local customs, etc., and use everything they have learned to scam other unsuspecting targets who thought the criminals were real people and lived in the same neighborhood and had shared customs. The scammers would reuse other victims' stolen photos and place them in their own profile, but the unsuspecting target has no clue the person they are talking to could be a team of scammers hiding under some fancy or attractive photos they have stolen. I have heard from some people in our support group that scammers have reused stolen pictures of their Christmas trees, plants, cars, and food. Like in many of our cases, the next target would not suspect anything unusual or out of the ordinary. Never in their wildest dreams would victims imagine that the charming and beautiful stranger they are chatting with is a carefully crafted persona being controlled by a criminal compound on the other side of the world. And within this compound is trafficked labor trapped in a cell where they are locked away for months or years while being forced to perpetrate these crimes under the threat of torture.

The PBS masterminds took advantage of the Covid-19 lockdowns knowing that people were feeling isolated and interacting more online to fill in the gap. They used these circumstances of financial upheaval and uncertainty to exploit their targets, who may either show interest in learning how to invest with cryptocurrency or persuade those with economic issues to do so. They took advantage of cryptocurrency's lack of government oversight and the irreversibility of transactions. I suspect that, during the Covid-19 pandemic, because the Chinese people were in lockdown and many did not have money to pour into these investment schemes or were already aware of the PBS going on there, criminals had to look elsewhere and began studying the daily lives of Americans and other wealthy countries. They analyzed how people had fared financially while many were unemployed. Criminals watch the news daily and may have heard that many Americans would receive stimulus checks. As a result, they figured they could feed off the Americans and wealthier countries, thinking they could steal some of this newly created wealth.

In the end, scammers will do anything in an attempt to manipulate your emotions and control your behavior. Most will play the victim card and fabricate stories to make you feel sorry for them. Most scripts create the persona of someone widowed (not only that, but their dead wife was two months pregnant!) or has experienced some deep trauma, such as still feeling scarred from a girlfriend who suddenly died in a car crash while on a video call. Members of our GASO support group have heard of just about every story or excuse in the book. If they are desperate, some scam companies will even invest in sending gifts such as flowers or (counterfeit) designer purses to reassure the victim they are real. When targets do not fall for the time pressure or sense of urgency and scammers are not able to accomplish what they set out for, they will begin gaslighting and guilt-tripping. All the while, they will try to obtain as much private information and as many photos (often nude photos) from the target in case they need to use extortion later should the target not follow their agenda by agreeing to invest in their cryptocurrency trading platform. Even if the targets did comply with using their trading platform, the perpetrators would still make up endless excuses why their funds could not be withdrawn. Either way, the perpetrators will profit off of their targets by selling their data to other scam companies or on the dark web and nude photos to porn sites. In some desperate cases, they will guilt victims with fake suicide attempts.

Even if you have lost all your money to the scammers, it may never seem enough to them as they will continue to attempt to scrape for every last bit. Some will ask you to borrow more money ("helpfully" providing step-by-step instructions), while others will try to squeeze every last cent out of you by pretending to be a crypto recovery company. In addition, we have seen scammers impersonating victims and infiltrating open online forums to target the next unsuspecting person. They will pose as a kind-hearted individual or organizations trying to help the next victim. It is a never-ending battle.

And even after you have already stopped communicating with the scammer, they will send you phishing texts and emails or try to open accounts under your stolen ID. To the scammers, you are their piggy bank, even if you have no money. The lesson here is never to undermine the scammers, as their hunger for your money is greater than your general understanding of greed and evil.

Unfortunately, if you have been scammed once, you are more likely to be a target later by other scammers.[6] I will discuss in Chapter 3 (What to do if you are a victim) the steps you should take to prevent yourself from becoming a victim again.

Again, it is a disgrace that so-called "reporters" shame victims for not being "careful" and ignorantly write-off their outcome as due to simple greed. This ignorance is an example of the "myth of the unmalleable mind"[5] at work and is what ensures the public's continued vulnerability to subtle yet powerful coercive persuasion techniques. Reporting on this topic presents an excellent opportunity to expose criminal masterminds. Reports and news media should be redirecting the issue of "greed" towards the powerful techniques of human persuasion that are being successfully weaponized by the perpetrators and masterminds rather than blaming the victims who were lured and manipulated into learning about a fake "investment" that they thought would provide a better future for their loved ones.

It will be a brutal fight to slow down and disrupt the cyber scam industry. When current methods are not giving the criminal masterminds the results they wish for, they will evolve and continue to find ways to scam people, even if it will come at the expense of other human lives. Human trafficking and abuse will continue if we are unable to halt the industry.

The PBS is the most brutal type of scam I have ever heard of. Even law enforcement is unprepared to handle this type of scam or unable to do anything because the criminals are scamming from overseas and continually change their URLs or websites in a game of whack-a-mole. They are always one step ahead and continuously adapt to changes as they study reports and alerts from GASO and other government agencies. Just about a month ago, in November 2022, scammers showed what they were capable of by hacking into a conference held by GASA.

As I am writing today, one of our newest GASO members has been victimized through her own inner circle of real-life friends. As we continue to spread awareness of the PBS and are doing what we can to try to slow down the scammers from preying on more people, scammers are now aiding overseas criminals by venturing and infiltrating groups of friends to conduct their crimes. Although her scam took on a different level of being victimized locally, she, like everyone else in our group, thought that because she is very cautious with money, she would never get scammed. This is an alert to remind everyone that it can, unfortunately, happen to anyone. Scammers can appear under the guise of just about anybody, including someone who you might think is a real-life friend.

My downfall was partly due to unknowingly throwing myself into the pack of wolves waiting for me while others had circumstances that pushed them into the situation involuntarily. It was reverse psychology when I used to assume that scammers only actively engage in trying to commit fraud on you. Again, little did I know that the pack of wolves that was waiting for me would show up under the guise of a decent, professionally looking profile along with a patient and polite human being who would spend weeks working to deliberately hijack my thoughts and actions through online chat. Because I was so used to being around men who were narcissistic and only focused on themselves, it seemed refreshing at the time to think that I had met someone who showed genuine care. I blame myself for naively falling for the deception and not noticing the red flags right away. Because I have not visited the internet and social media much in the past decade, I had forgotten about the dangers of online predators. Having been trained for years to watch out for scams such as phishing emails and the infamous Nigerian prince, I thought I was prepared never to get scammed.

Update:

There was a man named Bilce Tan who was brave enough to risk his life and was lucky enough to have escaped a compound in Cambodia where he was unwillingly forced to work. He had lost everything, including his wife, due to all the scammers' coercive persuasion. As a result of his cell phone being confiscated, the scammers were able to empty out all his bank accounts and erase all his data on the phone so that he no longer had any evidence against them. They erased all the memory in his cloud storage, too. Regardless, the victim put up a good fight and showed himself in the media to spread awareness about these human atrocities. Sadly, the company that had offered him employment is now suing him for going public with his story.[7,8] It is his words against theirs without having a shred of evidence. Fortunately, he did send some photos to his friend while trapped in the compound, so his friend may have evidence to support his case. I pray for Bilce's safety and for justice to prevail.

CHAPTER 2

THE AFTERMATH

- Disbelief, Shock, Devastation
- Panic, Distress, Anger
- Depression, Helplessness, Hopelessness
- Suicidal Ideation
- Shame, Blame, Guilt
- Self-doubt, Lost of trust, and Betrayal
- Isolation, Heartbreak, Despair
- Loss of financial security, Anxiety

Life savings gone, retirement gone and you're in debt... What now?

Just as with any victim's first reaction after discovering the scam, you feel complete utter shock and disbelief. You are completely devastated by what has just happened. Your entire life savings, retirement savings, inheritance, or loans used to fund your account had completely vanished in a moment's time. You have butterflies in your stomach, a sinking feeling in your chest, and shivers down your spine.

You go into panic mode. Your heart is pounding fast, and you may feel like hyperventilating. You suddenly lose your appetite. You are so distressed and distraught that you cannot eat or sleep for days and months. You struggle to wake up in the mornings. You cannot think or concentrate on your work or anything else.

You cannot control your anger from what has just happened. You want to scream your lungs out. You throw out all the cuss words you've ever possibly known from your vocabulary. You bang the walls to let your frustration out.

You lose enjoyment of the most basic things in life that once brought you joy. You sink into depression. You feel helpless and so overwhelmed with the feeling of hopelessness that you sink into severe depression and even have thoughts about killing yourself.

You might try to come up with ways to end your life as a result of all these negative emotions. But you stepped back for a second and knew you couldn't. You know you are an intelligent person who just got duped by psychological manipulation, and you figure there must be a way to fight back and find justice. Your days and nights now only involve tracing back to how the ordeal started. You keep replaying the crime in your head and what you could have done differently. You cannot perform simple tasks because your mind is paralyzed and stuck back in time.

You don't want to talk to a single soul. You fear that if you tell anyone, you will get blamed for your action, so you suck it up and stay silent. Your spouse, children, other family members, or friends have no idea why you behave the way you do, except they notice you are more quiet or cranky than usual, and you are just not your normal self. You are utterly frustrated that you let your guard down, and you feel guilt and shame that you contributed to your own victimization due to your lack of clear judgment or discernment at the time you were being psychologically manipulated. You feel responsible for everything that has happened and keep blaming yourself for all the events that led to your mess. You are embarrassed and ashamed, and you feel stupid.

You now start to doubt yourself. You lose confidence in your own judgment and lose trust in others. You've been wronged and betrayed by another human being. You withdraw from friends and family and go into isolation mode because you'd rather suffer in silence than risk having your family members, friends, or colleagues judge or put you down.

You are completely heartbroken for being played. Everything was a lie. Your hopes of finding that perfect person or securing your financial future are completely shattered. The wound is so deep you can never imagine ever being able to heal it. You are in complete despair.

You fear for your future and lose all sense of financial security. You develop anxiety and are in constant overdrive mode, worrying about every move you make next and how you will be able to support yourself and your family. You have mood swings that sometimes can seem out of control. You lack security in this world and feel damaged self-worth.

However, on the surface, you try your best to appear like an average person going about your everyday life. But deep down, you are struggling to survive. Your emotions eat you up. You want to scream and share with the world what you just went through, but you can't. There are so many reasons why you won't. What if people will unfairly judge you without knowing every detail of the events that led you to where you are? You bottled up everything inside. Then you feel like a ticking time bomb if someone says the wrong thing to you even though that person has no idea what they said might offend you or bring back the traumatizing memories. As a result of this traumatizing event, you will never be the same person again. You strongly feel, though, that you would never want this to happen to anyone else. While still very emotionally and financially distressed, you wonder who you can talk to and how you will ever be able to move on.

I know all these emotions because I have been there. After going through the roller coaster ride of every possible human emotion and difficulty sleeping and eating through the first few weeks post-scam, I wasn't sure how much longer I should continue living my life under a shell. I hated always making excuses why I couldn't go anywhere, do anything with anyone, or eat out the same way I used to. When I finally briefly let in one person about the traumatic loss, but still not fully admitting that I was scammed, I was advised to contact law enforcement. In a way, I was really glad that I disclosed my loss to that one person because it seemed like the advice I received was very sound, as I could not have even thought about it at the time it happened.

So, as I have shared in my personal story, I called the police. However, since the crime I would be reporting was not considered a priority, I had to wait two hours before a policeman decided to take my report. He gave me a pamphlet issued by the FBI and advised me to make a report on their Internet Crime Complaint Center website called IC3. That was the first time I had heard of that department. After completing my reports, I went through a lonely and quiet post-scam journey. I had no one I felt comfortable talking to about my scam and bottled up everything inside. That all changed when I eventually decided to contact GASO. When I finally joined GASO's USA peer support group, I realized I was not alone. So many members shared similar stories, and we learned that the PBS was victimizing many unsuspecting people and even taking many lives worldwide. I greatly appreciate the founder of GASO for her tremendous efforts in building the organization from scratch in the name of providing support to PBS victims like me and herself.

At the time our scams unfolded in 2021, there was hardly any news reporting or articles written on the PBS. I had never seen any media coverage of it. Internet searches in English did not yield any results for the type of crime that matched the description of what PBS victims had gone through. Knowing how devastating the effect of the scam had on the victims, GASO worked hard to contact law enforcement, news media, and journalists to alert the public about what was going on, as these scammers were popping up like weeds everywhere. However, the number of victims joining GASO kept growing rapidly worldwide. We felt if these scammers are not caught or deterred, more and more unsuspecting people will continue to fall prey. Now, in 2022, through the help of GASO and their members who were brave to quickly share their stories, more reports and news coverage on the PBS have been aired, and as a result, people are slowly becoming aware.

Sadly, however (and despite the warnings and alerts GASO has been sharing through media), many people will continue to have the mindset that "it will not happen to me," and we only pray that no one will ever get scammed. Unfortunately for all of the members of the GASO group, we have never heard of the PBS, and nearly 100% of victims admitted to having the same mindset before discovering their scam. Everyone confided that they have been very careful their whole life, especially with their hard-earned money, and firmly thought they were educated enough never to get scammed. But in the end, each member had unsuspectingly fallen for the lies and psychological manipulations of the scammers and was shocked to find out they had become another statistic.

Members in our USA GASO peer support group have already been drained in the tens of millions of dollars. This number comes from just the people who were vetted into the group and willing to speak up about their experience. Many in our group have also chatted with victims from other websites and forums, such as Reddit, who were too afraid to report their loss or join support groups or just wanted to move on. In addition, members from GASO and other sites reported knowing someone personally who also got scammed but did not want to disclose it to anyone or any organizations as well. As we know of the underreporting, the statistics should be higher than what has been officially recorded.

| DO NOT FALL FOR THE SAME TRAP!

You must learn not to fall for scammers twice. Remember that they are relentless in attempting to squeeze out every last drop of juice out of you. Even if there is a possibility that the scammer you have been talking to may be human trafficked, never fall for the trap of giving more money to "rescue" them even if they confess their "real love" for you or are in dire trouble and need to be rescued. Instead, report to GASO immediately and leave the rescue efforts to the authorities. There have been victims who, after discovering their scams, still have feelings for their scammers and wonder if their feelings were reciprocal. Chances are, the person you have been communicating with is not the same person you see in pictures or videos they share. Instead, the perpetrator may be a team of recruits rotating turns, or their supervisor, talking to you. You must detach yourself and stop communicating with your scammer.

To avoid falling into more traps, always be on alert. The perpetrators who have successfully stolen money from you may very well be the same people behind fake recovery companies posing to help victims. There have been victims who have fallen prey twice as a result of attempting to recover their money through fraudulent recovery companies. These illegitimate recovery companies will demand an upfront fee and use various terms such as "retainer fee" or "processing fee" to justify such charges. Many of these fraudulent recovery companies will register in the USA or the United Kingdom but, in reality, are hiding in the same regions as the fraud perpetrators. Always be suspicious and do not believe everything you read online, especially on forums or websites where anyone can openly post. Amongst the victims posting questions and seeking help are the scammers and perpetrators themselves, posing as victims and making up fake stories about how they had used recovery companies to help them retrieve their funds.

Additionally, there are individuals out there who claim to be professional hackers. Word of caution: do not hire hackers! They are another group of scammers looking to steal your money. They will feed off your desperation and provide false hope of getting your money back.

Also, never trust big exchanges to watch your back because this is how most victims fall for the trap to begin with. They trusted that since the money they put in was to known and popular exchanges, such as Coinbase and Crypto.com, they would be doing legitimate business with other crypto trading companies. Sadly, this is far from the truth. These exchanges only charge you excessively to use their platform, regardless of who is on the other receiving end. There is no regulation yet to stop them from working with fraudulent companies.

On the other hand, there are also private investigators, third-party services, and legitimate companies that can trace your blockchain. However, attempting to use these services may be fruitless as they are limited in what they can do to help recover your funds. Without the assistance of law enforcement and court orders, they will not be able to freeze and seize your assets. For the high price you will be paying, the most you may end up with is a crypto tracing report.

With the very few legitimate third-party recovery services out there, you will find yourself dealing with a very aggressive sales team that uses sales tactics to pressure you to hire them. They can charge anywhere from a few thousand to tens of thousands to justify the need to pay for their administration and operating costs. Their recovery method through connections overseas is to pressure scammers to give back the money. But the chances of them ever successfully recovering your money are very slim. Even if they recover your money after a very long period of waiting, which can usually be years, the amount would be minimal due to the extreme money laundering, which leaves a tiny percent of what you had initially invested. If the third-party services eventually retrieve your money and take a percentage of the cut, you are left with barely any money. The bottom line is, it is probably not worth your time or money to engage in third-party services.

As a reminder, be alert and do not get caught off-guard by anyone posing to help. Do not fork out any more money in an attempt to recover your stolen money. Never share your personal information, such as bank account numbers, usernames, passwords, or IDs, with someone who may be posing as a recovery company. Also, never send money orders, checks, or gift cards to an unfamiliar individual pretending to try to help you recover your funds. And as a rule of thumb, you must go directly to the official business website to make payments but never through a link sent to you by email, text, or on any other apps. Lastly, if your scammer has your identification and photos, they may be sold on the dark web to other potential scammers. These are legitimate reasons for increased concern about your safety and that of your family (I will discuss what you can do to protect yourself better in the next chapter).

In the US, crimes must be reported to law enforcement. Once you discover the crime, you are to report it to your local law enforcement, the FBI's Internet Crime Complaint Center-IC3, and several other agencies, which I will also go over in the next chapter. Other countries will have different regulations and policies. Please refer to your country's policies on reporting cyber or cryptocurrency fraud crimes. For example, in Europe, it would be through their national police agencies. In other countries, it is best to report in person.

It is ok and normal for you to vent and experience severe anxiety after everything you have gone through. Unfortunately, some victims have lost not just their entire life savings but also their homes and cars. As one victim had described, it is a "life-crushing and soul-crushing" experience. But remember, after the storm, there will be a rainbow. You may be going through your darkest days, but there will be light at the end of the tunnel. So please do not give up and know the storm will pass.

Meanwhile, learn to control your anger and not let it control you. Unmanaged anxiety and anger can negatively impact your health in the short and long term. Try to listen to motivational podcasts.

Do not project your anger or frustration onto other people, including your family, friends, or coworkers. Do not give your time and energy to people who have wronged you and save it for the better things in life. It is ok to be angry but spend your energy on physical activities such as boxing or playing ball to release all that negative energy. Or you can direct your anger towards a piece of paper or book. Write down all the things you need to say to the scammer, and everyone involved in your crime on paper, then burn all the pages once you have let all your thoughts and frustrations out. Or you can write your thoughts on some old plates and throw them in a designated area so that no one would get hurt. You can also go to a river and throw rocks. I will go over different things you can do to help with the healing process in Chapter 4 (Healing and Recovery).

But the first thing you need to do in the next day or two is report to as many agencies as possible. In the next chapter, I will guide you to the agencies you should prioritize reporting to and ways to protect yourself from future fraud. By reporting, not only will you have on record that you have become a scam victim, but you will play an essential role in alerting authorities to issue warnings and spread awareness of current scam trends.

In Chapter 4, I have put together some steps you can follow to help manage your feelings and begin the process of emotional and financial healing. However, if you are suffering from severe anxiety or emotional stress that cannot be managed, please seek professional help.

If you or someone you know are still in severe emotional distress or having thoughts of suicide or self-harm, please know that you are not alone, and there are resources out there available 24/7 (24 hours a day and 7 days a week) that can provide help. These resources will provide free and confidential support as you can call in anonymously.

National Suicide Prevention Lifeline: dial **800-273-TALK (8255)** or **988**.

Suicide & Crisis Lifeline or Crisis Text Hotline: Text "**HOME**" to **741741** or chat online through their website: *https://www.crisistextline.org/*.

CHAPTER 3

WHAT TO DO IF YOU ARE A VICTIM

Keep in mind that this book is written in 2022, when PBS stories are still fairly new and underreported, and law enforcement are slowly working together to fight the crime with the pieces of puzzles they are being given. The wishful thinking is that when law enforcement gets more reports and gain more experience with scams such as the PBS, some policies might change to assist future victims better. But for now, I've outlined what we can currently do with the resources we have. With all the reporting going on this year, we hope to see new processes come into effect to deter crypto fraud schemes and money laundering, seize funds and make arrests. Even if it may not ultimately result in recovering your lost money, at least you will be able to help promote awareness with as much reporting as you can do and hopefully prevent others from falling prey.

Even if you are unsure why you should file with the police or FBI because you feel they might not do anything, you should still report the crime immediately. It may come in handy later if you need evidence to support your case, such as if you ever need to go to court or file for tax relief/IRS audits, bankruptcy, etc.

1. REPORT THE CRIME

(If you live outside the United States, please contact your local law enforcement for guidance on how or where to file the crime and your complaints.)

These are the agencies you should report to if you live in the United States: Local Police, IC3, USSS, REACT, FTC, CFTC, CFPB, SEC, BBB, DFPI

To prioritize, you should immediately file your case with the local Police, FBI/IC3, REACT & USSS. If you report immediately or within 48hrs and these agencies are able to hop on your case right away, they may be able to trace your wallets, freeze, or seize your stolen funds. There are also other agencies that offer their service to trace your wallets. However, many are limited in what they can do for you without the involvement of law enforcement. Be extra careful when you solicit third-party recovery companies, as most are just after your upfront fees. Currently, the only chance of making any actual recoveries depends on police seizure orders and cooperation from cryptocurrency exchanges.

As soon as you can, also report to GASO, your banks, FTC, CFTC, CFPD, SEC, BBB, and DFPI in a timely manner.

The USA Gov website *https://www.usa.gov/stop-scams-frauds#item-35157* allows you to report scams and frauds through various links to get you to some of the agencies listed above, such as FTC, IC3, and attorney general.

If you can, contacting your local politicians, State Attorney General, Governor, Senator, and Representative may help get the word out about these crimes. The more agencies you report to, the more public awareness can be made. However, it may be more effective to get the word out to your politicians if you collaborate with as many victims as possible and collectively sign a petition requesting for change in how banks and cryptocurrency exchanges should operate to protect consumers better.

If you want to try to trace where your funds went, you can also do independent searching by inputting your wallet into one of these websites:

https://ethplorer.io/
https://www.blockchain.com/explorer
https://www.walletexplorer.com/
https://bitcoinwhoswho.com/
https://oxt.me/

GASO has a very good article detailing how to trace your money to the final wallet. You can visit this article at:

https://www.globalantiscam.org//post/step-by-step-crypto-trace-guidebook-to-the-big-boss-final-wallet-by-iidi

POLICE

Police: The method of filing with the police varies depending on where you live. Check to see if you can file online or need to submit your report in person.

If you have given your personal identification, such as your driver's license or passport, to the scam website, report it immediately to your police and try to get them replaced if possible, to avoid any new accounts or fraudulent activity being opened in your name.

A website that you can use to search for a police or sheriff department near you is:

https://www.searchquarry.com/police-and-sheriff-department-finder/

Make sure you receive a copy of your report in case you ever need it to go to court or for filing your taxes. You do not want to be accused of fraud should you try to write off your taxes without any evidence or go to a court hearing where maybe your spouse thinks you are hiding money.

FEDERAL BUREAU OF INVESTIGATION (FBI)

https://www.fbi.gov

Headquarters:
935 Pennsylvania Ave, NW
Washington D.C. 20535-0001
202-324-3000

IC3 (Internet Crime Complaint Center): report online at *https://www.ic3.gov* or by phone 800-225-5324

FBI has a federal agency called IC3 where you can report internet crimes to. Per their website, an "Internet Crime" can include any illegal activity involving websites, chat rooms and/or emails. Examples of these crimes can include employment or business opportunity schemes or non-delivery of goods or services.

IC3 collects reports of fake websites, emails, malware, and other internet scams. If you have been affected by an international scam, report it through econsumer.gov. Your report will help offices spot trends and prevent scams.

The more thorough, accurate, and complete your complaint, the better IC3 can process your information and disperse it to the appropriate federal, state, local or international law enforcement or regulatory agencies for criminal, civil, or administrative action as appropriate.

IC3's Recovery Asset Team has assisted in freezing hundreds of thousands of dollars for victims of cybercrime.[1]

Just note that the IC3 center is for collecting information only, so you will not hear from them directly, as information will be investigated through receiving agencies.

Currently, there are 56 field offices across the United States and Puerto Rico.

Addresses and phone numbers can be found on their website: *https://www.fbi.gov/contact-us/field-offices*

FBI also has special agents stationed overseas. There are about 250 special agents stationed worldwide.

If you are grouped and given a case #, you will be mailed a letter stating that you are registered and will be given access to the Victim Notification System (*https://www.notify.usdoj.gov/*) where you can check on the status of your case. Unfortunately, not all victims may receive this.

UNITED STATES SECRET SERVICE (USSS)

https://www.secretservice.gov

US Secret Service
245 Murray Ln SW Bldg T-5
Washington D.C. 20223
202-406-5708

USSS is an agency of the United States Department of Homeland Security that investigates the complex, cyber-enabled financial crime against the U.S. financial system that is committed by criminals around the world.

Their mission is to protect and do financial investigations to ensure the safety and security of protectees, key locations and events of national significance, and the integrity of the U.S. currency.

USSS works with local, state, federal, and international law enforcement agencies and private sectors.

USSS may be the closest to the best support we have right now as they can freeze wallets and are continually learning and coming up to speed with the current scams.

Currently, there are 46 locations listed on their website. You can find a list of field offices in the US by visiting their website: *https://www.secretservice.gov/contact/field-offices.*

RAPID ENFORCEMENT ALLIED COMPUTER TEAM (REACT)

http://www.reacttf.org

70 West Hedding St West Wing
San Jose, CA 95110
408-282-2420
Fax 408-282-2421

If you live in the California Bay Area, there is a special task force called REACT that you should immediately seek assistance from to help freeze your assets if they are still in your account. However, you do not need to be a resident of California to seek their help.

REACT: an alliance of local, state, and federal law enforcement officials whose task force was formed to combat high technology crime (white-collar, money laundering, identity theft, intellectual property theft, etc.) and threats they pose to the health and welfare of the public and private communities.

They work with local, state, and federal agencies to increase recovery rates of stolen cryptocurrency by investigating, prosecuting a wide range of criminal offenders, arresting, freezing, and seizing assets.

They do not take crime reports, though.

The only REACT task force contacts I could find were Rick Jenkins & Erin Nordby West.

Rick Jenkins is a detective with the Gilroy Police Department.

Erin Nordby West is the current Deputy District Attorney-Cybercrime and Crypto Prosecutor in Santa Clara County.

According to Erin West, victims across the nation and even the world have flooded their office with PBS cases. At the same time, Rick Jenkins confirms that their office has been receiving multiple cases a week within the past year nonstop.[2]

So far, the REACT taskforce has been the most proactive and best support we have seen for PBS victims with several successful cases of seizing and returning stolen assets to the victims. We hope to see more local and federal agencies follow their footstep in acting quickly to help victims recover their money and disrupt the cyber scam industry.

FEDERAL TRADE COMMISSION (FTC)

https://www.ftc.gov

Federal Trade Commission
600 Pennsylvania Ave, NW
Washington DC 20580
202-326-2222

FTC: report any types of scams online through the FTC Complaint website at: *https://reportfraud.ftc.gov* or by phone at 877-382-4357

To report identity theft, report at: *https://www.identitytheft.gov* or phone at 877-IDTHEFT (877-438-4338), 9am-8pm ET.

FTC is the national clearinghouse for consumer complaints. They are the main agency that collects scam and identity theft reports, spot trends, and issue warnings to the public. They will accept complaints about most scams and regularly update their websites with scam alerts. Your report will be shared with more than 3,000 law enforcers.

Their mission is to protect consumers by preventing deceptive and unfair business practices through law enforcement, advocacy, and education.

Like the FBI, FTC does not resolve individual cases but uses the reports to investigate and bring cases against fraud, scams, and bad business practices.

Currently, there are eight regional offices located in: Atlanta, Chicago, Cleveland, Dallas, Los Angeles, New York, San Francisco, Seattle

COMMODITY FUTURES TRADING COMMISSION (CFTC)

https://cftc.gov

Three Lafayette Centre
1155 21st Street, NW
Washington, DC 20581
202-418-5000
fax 202-418-5975
TTY 202-418-5428

You can fill out the Tips/Complaints/Referral (TCR) form online at: *https://www.cftc.gov/complaint* or call the toll-free Consumer Assistance and Complaints hotline at 866-FON-CFTC (866-366-2382)

CFTC: this is the agency under FBI responsible for managing cryptocurrency-related topics and future commodities and identifying money mules.

Their mission is to promote integrity, resilience, and vibrancy of US derivatives markets through sound regulation.

Report any information about a violation of the Commodity Exchange Act or Commission regulating any suspicious activities to the Division of Enforcement by submitting either Whistleblower form (TCR) or a Complaint form.

There are currently three regions:

Central:
77 West Jackson Blvd., Suite 800
Chicago, IL 60604
312-596-0700
fax 312-596-0716
TTY 312-596-0565

Southwestern:
2600 Grand Boulevard, Suite 210
Kansas City, MO 64108
816-960-7700
fax 816-960-7750
TTY 816-960-7704

Eastern:
290 Broadway, 6th Floor
New York, NY 10007
646-746-9700
fax 646-746-9888
TTY 646-746-9820

Customer Protection line:
202-418-5250 File a Complaint with our Reparations Program
866-366-2382 Report Suspicious Activities or Information to
the CFTC

U.S. SECURITIES AND EXCHANGE COMMISSION (SEC)

https://www.sec.gov

Headquarters:
100 F Street, NE
Washington DC 20549

File a complaint with SEC about any fraudulent investment or investment account, including Ponzi or Pyramid schemes, high yield investment programs, theft or misappropriation of funds, and insider trading.

Submit any tips, complaints, and referrals (TCRs) online at: *https://www.sec.gov/tcr*.

SEC's mission is to protect investors. Their job is to maintain fair, orderly, and efficient markets and promote a market environment worthy of the public's trust.

SEC has the power to register, regulate, and oversee brokerage firms. In addition, they issue alerts on investment fraud and scams.

CONSUMER FINANCIAL PROTECTION BUREAU (CFPB)

https://www.consumerfinance.gov

CFPB: US government agency whose mission is to ensure you are treated fairly by banks, lenders, and other financial institutions. They submit complaints about financial products and services to companies for a response which are then published in the Consumer Complaint Database after the company responds. Per the CFPB website, 98% of complaints sent to companies get timely responses.

Address to Mail a Complaint:
Consumer Financial Protection Bureau
PO Box 27170
Washington DC 20038
855-411-2372
TTY/TTD 855-729-2372
8am to 8pm E.T. Mon-Fri

Address for Other Correspondence:
Consumer Financial Protection Bureau
1700 G St NW
Washington DC 20552

BETTER BUSINESS BUREAU (BBB)

https://www.bbb.org

4250 North Fairfax Dr., Suite 600
Arlington, VA 22203
703-276-0100
General inquiries: 408-278-7400

BBB: a private organization that provides the public with information on businesses and charities.

The mission is to be the leader in advancing marketplace trust by encouraging best practices by engaging with and educating consumers and businesses.

You can file a complaint or report a scam or search for a business. BBB gives a business 14 days to respond to a complaint before sending a follow-up letter.

Through the recent uptick in reports from victims, the Better Business Bureau has issued alerts to consumers to be aware of elaborate cryptocurrency scams.

DEPARTMENT OF FINANCIAL PROTECTION & INNOVATION (DFPI)

https://www.dfpi.ca.gov

Main Office:
2101 Arena Blvd
Sacramento, CA 95834
916-445-7205
866-275-2677

If you live in California, you can report to DFPI.

DFPI: provides protections to consumers, borrowers, and investors engaged in financial transactions. They evaluate and review complaints and take appropriate actions when they find laws are violated. They can do such by filing civil actions and obtaining restitution for consumers. They can also charge penalties against violators.

You can file complaints if you feel that a financial service provider is using unlawful, unfair, abusive, or deceptive practices.

For a faster response, file online at *https://dfpi.ca.gov/file-a-complaint/*.

During the complaint process, DPFI will facilitate communication between consumers and financial institutions.

Currently, there are 4 locations: Sacramento, San Francisco, Los Angeles, and San Diego

For general inquiries, you can call toll-free at 866-275-2677 or 916-327-7585.

You can contact them through email at: *Ask.DFPI@dfpi.ca.gov.*

GLOBAL ANTI-SCAM ORGANIZATION (GASO)

https://www.globalantiscam.org

From my personal experience, reporting to GASO is probably one of the most beneficial actions you can take. It is one of the most resourceful organizations to seek help from as it is run by volunteers who have been scam victims themselves and therefore understand what you are going through and genuinely care and want to help you.

After you report to the GASO website, a dedicated volunteer will help direct you to the proper resources for help, depending on your case.

They can help trace your wallet, use the information you provided, and try to group your case together with other victims.

GASO has already collected and blacklisted thousands of scam websites. By reporting to them, you can help them continue to spread awareness of the growing scams.

Victims can play an important role here by volunteering their time and skills to help with the fight against scammers. In addition, they can contact the media or journalists to help spread the word or write articles and stories to post on the website.

One important thing to remember is that GASO is run solely on donations. Due to a lack of funding right now, they are limited in what they can do compared to if they were sufficiently funded to run their operation more efficiently.

STATE ATTORNEYS GENERAL

https://www.usa.gov/state-attorney-general

Attorney generals are the top legal officers in their state. Their job is to act as the "people's lawyer."

SAO (State Attorney's Office): just like FTC, they keep track of reported fraud and scams within your state and issue public announcements to warn others and provide tips.

You may file a complaint with the Attorney General's Consumer Protection Division:

Consumer Protection Division
P.O. Box 30213
Lansing, MI 48909
517-335-7599
Toll-free 877-765-8388
Fax 517-241-3771

Or you can report your crime to the Cyber Crime Division at your state's attorney general office.

You can also contact the White House switchboard at 202-456-1414 or the comments line at 202-456-1111 during business hours.

For congressional representatives and senators, you can search the websites below to see who represents your district. It should be their job to assist the citizens in their district to escalate issues to federal government agencies.

GOVERNOR

https://www.usa.gov/state-governor

SENATOR

https://www.senate.gov/senators/senators-contact.htm

UNITED STATES HOUSE OF REPRESENTATIVES

https://www.house.gov/representatives

2. TALK TO YOUR BANK AND CRYPTO EXCHANGE

Contact your bank and exchange as soon as possible after discovering that you have been scammed. There is no guarantee that you will get your money back, but the least you can do is try to talk to them, tell them what happened, that you were a victim of a scam, and request to start a fraud investigation as soon as possible.

Do not close your bank account right away if you plan on opening a dispute and request your bank to reverse any fraudulent transactions. However, if you provided your account information to the scammer, it may be advisable to close your account immediately and open a new one.

When attempting to talk to your bank and exchange, make sure you provide all records, including transaction dates and amounts. Inform them you have reported to the police and FBI and explain that you found out the crypto trading platform is responsible for your loss when you were unable to withdraw.

Be patient, as the investigation can take months. If you are unhappy with the initial response, try to appeal through a different form of communication, such as email or a letter. That way, your communication is all documented.

Per the GASO website, several US and UK victims have received small bank refunds after sending letters.

Banks and exchanges could do more to help prevent their consumers from being scammed, especially when they see large sums of money being transferred out. They should be inquiring you about the purpose of investment and if you have validated the trading exchange to be trustworthy or at least raise a red flag if they have any suspicion the consumer may possibly be getting scammed.

It would not hurt for victims to collectively make some noise and alert banks and politicians about the lack of protection for consumers. Even though the victim authorized the transactions, the victim would not have known that the money would ultimately end up in the scammer's pockets under the guise of licensed companies. Otherwise, they would have never transferred the money out to begin with.

3. FREEZE CREDIT BUREAUS AND LOCK SOCIAL SECURITY

If your scammer has a copy of your ID, social security, or any personal identifying information, such as your date of birth, make sure you reach out to the credit bureaus. Let them know you have been a victim of fraud and request to put a freeze on your credit so if the scammer wants to open up a fraudulent account in your name, they would not be able to obtain a new line of credit such as a loan or credit card. The freeze on credit reports will prohibit anyone from viewing your credit report unless you unfreeze it.

The three national credit bureaus are Experian, TransUnion, and Equifax.

Experian: 888-397-3742 / Fraud Dept: 888-397-3742

TransUnion: 800-916-8800 / Fraud Dept: 800-680-7289

Equifax: 888-378-4329 / Fraud Dept: 800-525-6285

Alternatively, you can also consider placing a free 90-day fraud alert on your credit reports instead if you do not want to go through the process with each credit bureau. With this request, you only need to reach out to one credit bureau, and the initial company will send the information to the other two bureaus. The initial fraud alert will remain on your credit reports for 90 days, and if you'd like, you can renew it as often as you want.

If you suspect your scammer has your social security number (SSN), you can request to block electronic access by calling the Social Security Administration at 800-772-1213 or creating an E-verify account. Locking your SSN will prevent further unauthorized use of it.

You can also report social security scams to the office of the Inspector General by calling the fraud hotline at 800-269-0271 or filing a report at *https://oig.ssa.gov/.*

4. INCREASE SECURITY

If applicable, report that your ID may be stolen and change it if possible.

Factory reset your phone in case your scammer might have installed any spyware on your phone.

Maintain unique accounts. Do not use the same user ID or passwords across multiple accounts.

Change passwords to your accounts. Make strong, complex passwords, and do not reuse the same passwords.

Set up two-step authentication (2FA) on apps so that accessing accounts will only be authorized once you allow it through your phone.

Check your credit score on a regular basis to monitor for any signs of fraudulent activity.

Never engage with but report or block any unwanted calls or text messages.

| 5. TALK TO A CPA OR TAX LAWYER

Talk to your CPA or tax lawyer to figure out how you will file your taxes for the following year. You will need to plan ahead and save all your documents for proof of information that you will submit on your return. Due to the unprecedented cases of theft resulting from PBS in the US, filing for crypto loss due to fraud or theft may be unclear and a gray area for many CPAs right now. Sadly, the only firms willing to comfortably do it for you will charge you an arm and a leg. So far, many victims in our support group who chose the route of claiming loss due to fraud or theft have been charged somewhere in the few thousands to file their returns. Until the laws for filing crypto loss are more defined for victims of the PBS, it will be challenging to find a CPA who can comfortably file for you due to the lack of experience since these scams are still relatively new here in the US. It is probably best to find a CPA that you can trust and who will defend you in case you do get audited by the IRS, which typically could be within three years of filing but more if they find a substantial error.

If you plan on claiming a loss due to fraud or theft of your crypto investment, make sure you file for the discovery year. For example, if you discovered your loss was in 2021 and plan on claiming that loss due to theft, you must file in 2022. If you try to file in 2023, it may be too late, and you may no longer be able to claim it. Again, since this is still a very new and a gray area, please consult with a CPA who is more knowledgeable in the crypto area and has confidence in working with the IRS on the chance that you are audited. It is very important to have your taxes done correctly. Otherwise, you might end up spending more money on fines, penalties, and interest for filing incorrectly.

It may also be a good idea to pay for audit defense.

However, if you choose not to file your loss and, therefore, not have to deal with the headaches of getting audited for the loss, you will be able to move on with a clean slate. You can start over and start saving up again.

If you do want to proceed with filing for the loss, remember to make sure you maintain all documents, including police and FBI reports, bank statements showing the money you transferred out to the exchange, screenshots of your transactions on the fraudulent trading form, and chats with your scammers that are relevant to leading to your loss.

6. EDUCATE YOURSELF

Educate yourself by learning how scammers may use psychological manipulations and persuasion to influence an unsuspecting person to comply with financial investment advice that may seem benign or non-maleficent.

Read up on all the latest fraud and scam alerts from government websites, especially from agencies whose mission is to protect consumers, such as the FBI, FTC, and CFPB.

Never act when you are put under pressure, which is a very common tactic scammers use to persuade their targets. Whether they present a problem, such as a threat or a deal too good to miss, they will create a sense of urgency for you to act before you have time to think. Resist that pressure to act on the spur of the moment, whether it is a response through email, text, online, phone, or in person.

By educating yourself, you may be able to recognize potential red flags more quickly than someone who has never heard or read about them.

If you are interested in doing some crypto investment or mining pool, try using this website: *https://whoisdog.com* to see if the business you are interested in is listed. Research how long the website has been around and be extremely wary of the more recent ones. If it is not recent or listed, you should do your due diligence to learn more about that business. It is especially important to talk to someone you trust and get a second or professional opinion before engaging in any investment activities that you are new to or unsure of.

Learn about the dangers of phishing emails and texts so that you do not accidentally click on links and accidentally fill out information that can reveal your personal and confidential information to scammers. Even if you feel the link may be sent from your work or an official business, go straight to the legitimate website to conduct any transactions. You do not want to open a can of worms by clicking on a link that is not from a legitimate business.

Ignore all spam text messages, app messages, and emails and mark them as spam.

Do not engage and never respond to what may seem like an accidental text or email.

| 7. FOCUS ON WHAT CAN BE DONE

In the next chapter: Healing and Recovery, I will do my best to go over ways you can heal financially and emotionally.

However, if working to pay off your debt is too overwhelming, please consult a financial advisor on the next step or best action plan. Speak to a non-profit counseling agency counselor first to see if they can help create a budget for you or recommend filing for bankruptcy. In the case filing for bankruptcy is recommended, you should consult with a bankruptcy attorney. The first sessions for consult should usually be free for both counselors and most attorneys.

For some victims like AM, filing for bankruptcy may be the last resort. Although there is a stigma associated with bankruptcy, filing for bankruptcy may allow you to start all over and rebuild your finances under the protection of bankruptcy laws.

Alternatively, if you feel that filing for bankruptcy is totally out of the question, research if your state offers hardship relief programs. It does not hurt to try to apply and see if you are qualified. Anytime you go online, proceed with caution to the websites you are entering. You should first verify if the websites are legitimate just to ensure you will not fall prey to another scam.

8. SEEK PROFESSIONAL HELP

If you feel overwhelmed and are not able to handle the stress as a result of this scam, please seek professional help. As mentioned at the end of Chapter 2, toll-free call centers are available 24/7, ready to answer the phone to assist you (dial 988 for the suicide hotline / text "HOME" to 741741 for the crisis text hotline). However, I hope that by absorbing what I will share in the next chapter, you can utilize what you have learned and move forward the best you can.

Please call 911 for immediate help if you feel your current situation is life-threatening or go to any hospital emergency room and ask for a psychiatric specialist. Depending on your insurance plan, you may be charged for any services rendered by the hospital.

9. TAKE A BREAK

After you have done everything that you possibly can to report, prevent further loss, and help spread awareness, give yourself a break. Learn to breathe again and allow yourself to begin the healing and recovery process.

CHAPTER 4

HEALING AND RECOVERY

HEALING IS POSSIBLE AND WILL TAKE TIME

As a disclaimer, I am no expert or have any experience with mental counseling or providing therapy to any person or group. However, after going through the process of my own healing and recovery, I feel that the information I have gathered and presented here can be helpful to PBS victims, especially those who cannot afford to seek professional counseling or access to professional help.

Please note that this book is in no way a substitute for professional counseling if needed. Please seek professional help if you are unable to find constructive advice here or have suicidal intentions.

As a scam victim, I know I cannot erase the past, and I wish there were a pill to erase the trauma. Just like in the American psychological thriller, "*Homecoming,*"[1] I wish I could also be given the memory-erasing medication to help eradicate my trauma through the process of deleting the memories. I would love to have some medicine sprinkled on my food so I would forget how I was manipulated into losing my entire life savings. However, ultimately, I realized that I had made a costly mistake by believing in the good intentions of other human beings who pretended to care. After understanding what goes on behind the scenes of the PBS, I also realize now that sometimes it may not even be the person who perpetrated the scam who is to blame.

Nevertheless, I was a victim, one of many who was ultimately slaughtered. I must understand that life does not always go as planned, no matter how good my intentions are. I will think of what happened to me as an expensive lesson.

What I have learned is that, with time and therapy, I will heal, recover, and move forward. You, too, will be able to do the same. As hard as it may feel when you realize that you've been "slaughtered" and your entire world has turned upside down, it is possible to heal and move forward, and you can become stronger in the end. I've learned that you must be kind to yourself before becoming whole again, but it will take some time and effort to get there. As with any loss in life, there will be a time when you will eventually be able to move on. No one says the recovery process will be easy, and no one can tell you how long it will take, but the time it takes to heal, and recover is ultimately up to you. The sooner you are able to move on, the better. You may never forget the trauma, but you can continue living, learning, taking care of your mind and body, and hopefully, making peace with yourself by releasing the blame and learning the positive affirmations for healing.

In this chapter, I will go over the two types of healing most victims need to recover: financial and emotional. What I've learned is that to heal properly post-scam, you must first have to acknowledge and accept the fact that you've been a victim at no fault of your own, understand the financial and emotional impact the scam has created, and be able to acknowledge that this scam can happen to anybody.

| FINANCIAL HEALING

From being overly cautious with money and having a comfortable savings to begin with, most PBS victims have suddenly been thrown into survival mode as a result of their abrupt loss. Immediately after being severed from your entire life savings, it may seem impossible to see beyond the loss that had just occurred. For many, this sudden and devastating loss can result in severe trauma. Financial trauma can understandably interfere with a person's ability to carry out routine work and life functions, as nagging thoughts of financial doom will undoubtedly interfere with the ability to focus and concentrate. For the general population, money can sometimes or oftentimes be interpreted as worthiness. This is far from the truth. Money should never be tied to your self-worth. Your self-worth should never be equated to your net worth. You are worth more than money or your relationship to practically anything outside your inner self, including your job, house, or car you drive. Self-worth should only be defined from within. So regardless of your job title, bank accounts, assets, or liabilities, you have inherent value as a human being. Please know that you are worthy just the way you are. The loss of money cannot and should never define your self-worth. Our life is worth a lot more than any amount of money the scammers can steal or has stolen from us.

Once you have grasped the understanding that your self-worth is not tied to the money you have or don't have, you may be able to heal financially with more grace. The first thing you will need to do in the aftermath of the scam is to create a plan for your future. The plan must be realistic so that you can have reachable goals. Once you have the plan in place, you can work your way toward the future. Three things you need to include in your plan are 1) work to reduce your debt, 2) seek help from family, friends, or professionals, and 3) make a new budget.

WORK TO REDUCE DEBT

Depending on the amount lost, which in the case of most PBS victims, would be their entire life savings and/or a large amount of debt, the length of time for financial recovery will vary for each person. While it may take some people a few years to recoup their loss, others might take a few decades or more. Unfortunately, for some, it may seem unfathomable to ever recoup their total loss. The huge financial loss will be a point in life where you will need to realign yourself with new goals and plans for your life. To achieve your goals, you must first take baby steps. Think about climbing steps on the ladder to get to the top. You cannot expect to be at the top without making the smaller steps first, so tackle one thing at a time.

The first thing you need to do is, if you have taken out a loan or loans, try to pay back the one with the highest interest first. Alternatively, if you took out a second loan and the balance on that loan is much smaller, you can try to pay that loan off first and get it out of the way sooner. Next, you might want to renegotiate your pay with your employer to see if you can receive a raise or try to work overtime to earn more. If overtime or a raise is out of the question or not sufficient, then you may want to take on a second or even third job to achieve the goal faster.

SEEK HELP FROM FAMILY, FRIENDS, OR A PROFESSIONAL

Another option would be to seek financial help from a close family member or friend you can confide in about the scam. If you borrowed money from a family or friend, talk to them about the scam and see if they can give you more time to pay them back. Chances are, if they understand your situation, they will be able to work with you and understand your struggle to pay them back right away.

If you took out several loans or a loan is too big for you to pay back in a timely manner, even after picking up a second or third job or seeking help from family members or friends, talk to a professional counselor for advice. Learn about all the options available before making any big decisions, such as filing for bankruptcy.

There are many sources out there that are available and free to everyone that you may want to utilize. Most credit counseling agencies are nonprofit. They can negotiate with creditors on your behalf to create an affordable debt management plan. They can help consolidate your debt and manage your finance. Make sure the help you receive is from a reputable debt relief company.

You can search for credit counselors through the National Foundation for Credit Counseling at *https://www.nfcc.org/* or Financial Counseling Association of America at *https://fcaa.org/find-a-credit-counselor/*.

Or you can call 211, a free social service program available 24/7 for emergencies and crises. It will not hurt to see if you qualify for assistance.

You can also see if you qualify for debt relief through National Debt Relief by visiting their website: *https://nationaldebtrelief.com*.

Some states have their own debt relief program. For example, in California, you can visit the website: https://*californiadebtrelief*.org.

If you are not qualified for debt relief, you might want to hire a bankruptcy attorney to help explain your rights and guide you through the process.

Some people in my support group were able to refinance or take money out of their homes to pay back the loans and therefore focused on paying back only their home loans. Others found themselves buried in debt they knew they just could not pay back and ended up filing for bankruptcy. There may be a stigma associated with bankruptcy but filing for bankruptcy may not necessarily be a bad thing, as it allows a chance for you to start all over. It does not mean you are a failure with money. The disadvantage, however, is bankruptcy will remain on your record for 7-10 years. During this time, your credit score can be adversely affected and may make it harder for you to obtain big loans such as a mortgage or car loan.

To learn more about debt relief and bankruptcy, you can call Debt.org at 866-612-9971 or visit their website at: https://www.*debt*.org/. There, you will find many different resources, answers to commonly asked financial questions, and available options.

Financial recovery is not easy, but there are options out there, so talk to a professional counselor and see which path may be best for you to move forward with.

CREATE A BUDGET

Lastly, to better plan for the future, you will need to create a new budget that is more realistic. You will need to separate your wants and needs into two categories. There are certain things that you need to spend money on that are necessities. Such expenses include rent or mortgage, utility bills, food, and transportation costs. List everything that is a necessity and cannot be negotiated in the first column of your budget. Everything else that is not on that list can be negotiated. Ask yourself, is this item necessary, and will removing it from your second column be detrimental to your health? If the answer is no, try removing that expense temporarily for one year.

An example could be Netflix or some subscription that is not necessary for home or work. Other examples could be the daily run to your favorite coffee shop, a weekly visit to your favorite restaurant, or biweekly manicures. Consider giving up shopping for clothes for a year and buying an outfit only if it would be beneficial for a new job interview. Try having a family member or friend cut your hair. Try washing your own car if you feel a wash is needed. Try going for a jog or walk with a friend in the park instead of spending money on movies or a drink.

If you need to buy something, try going to a thrift store or buying less expensive brand items. But remember to ask yourself, do you really need this, or is it just a want? If it is a want, you can mark it down on your wish list to buy later after you have paid back your loans and saved up enough money, or maybe wait for a special occasion to treat yourself. Many stores have free rewards programs that will occasionally give you discounts if you subscribe to them. Although it may be a lot of work to track down all the services or programs you've joined, the discounts can come in handy when you need them. For example, when I needed to shop for clothes for my children, I signed up for the free rewards program at the Children's Place. Once enrolled as a member, I would receive free shipping anytime and coupons every now and then. If I wanted to shop at Amazon, I would try to see if a family member could add me to their household account so that I could receive free shipping. Currently, Amazon allows up to two adults per household account.

When going to work or events, try to pack your own food. Plan ahead and buy only what you need. Make a list of what you would like to eat for the whole week and shop for those food without buying anything in excess that may end up in waste. Also, make sure when selecting perishable items, such as milk, to look for the longest expiration date so they don't spoil too fast. Cook in large quantities so you can make more portions to last you a few days. Pack those food for lunch or events as well as your own water or drinks. You can easily save a few extra dollars every time you do so. If you want to dine out, research restaurants that give discounts on certain hours, such as happy hour, or on days that are usually not so busy such as Tuesday or Thursday. Ask if they have any promotions or discounts for certain people in your group with different age ranges such as the elder or children. When I want to dine out, I would also sign up for rewards programs at restaurants. I am fortunate to find some restaurants near me, such as TGIF, IHOP, and Denny's, that provide free or discounted meals for your birthday or occasional discounts such as 20% off your entire meal. Some of these restaurants also have promotions where kids can eat for free or the elderly at a discounted price on specific days during non-peak hours. By taking advantage of these programs, you can continue to save a little bit and enjoy yourself once in a while. If you plan on buying coffee, tea, or smoothie at your favorite shop because it's too good to replicate at home, also try to see if they have a rewards program there. I've happily utilized the free rewards program at Starbucks, Jamba Juice, and some tea shops. Usually, with the rewards program, every purchase adds up, and you can earn free drinks as you go.

You can further cut down your expenses by making some small adjustments to your essential spending as well. For example, you can reduce your utility bills by being more conservative. To save money on your water bill, you can cut down on your shower times, make sure you do not let the water run while brushing your teeth or wash fuller loads of laundry versus less in one setting. If you have a garden, trees, or plants, try watering them in the early morning to ensure optimum absorption and utilization of the water. Water is a very precious commodity and continues to be a limited resource as we have been through several years of drought. So, by maintaining the maximum benefits of less evaporation before the sun goes down, not only are you wasting less water and conserving this precious resource, but you will also be saving money by cutting down on its use. If it is inconvenient for you to water in the morning, then do it at night but avoid mid-day. Also, cut down on the number of days you water your plants to once every three to four days instead of every day or other day. When doing dishes, try using an energy-efficient dishwasher if you have one instead of handwashing yourself. Many new dishwashers can yield the same clean dishes with a fraction of the water you would normally use when handwashing yourself. There are also many different ways to save on your electric bills. When doing laundry, try to avoid washing or drying during peak hours as your electric bill will be higher then. Your electric company will usually charge less in the late evening to early morning so try doing laundry between those hours to minimize your bill. Other ways to save can include turning off appliances when you are not using them, such as lights, TV, or your computer when you're away for a while. Use energy-efficient appliances and light bulbs or LED lights to drain less energy. Adjust your thermostat during the hot and cold seasons so that they are not running all day, but you are still able to maintain optimum temperatures and be comfortable when you are at home. Using a programmable thermostat should help decrease your worry about high consumption when you are away. Use more blankets and wear warm socks in the wintertime, and if possible, reinforce your home's insulation. Lower your hot water temperature so that you use fewer kilowatts, and use cold water, if possible, for most of your laundry.

With the way inflation has been affecting so many households and rising gas prices eating up your wallet fast, you should continue to try to find more ways to save money. Another example would be to cut down on gas consumption for your car or find a way to save money at the gas pumps. Again, if you sign up for the free rewards program at the gas stations, most places should be able to give you a discounted price on gas if you are a member. You will also get better discounts if you pay by cash versus using a credit card. When you drive, begin by accelerating slowly and watch your speed, as driving too fast tends to waste more gas. Try not to let your car idle if not necessary. Plan your daily routes ahead of time so that you run your errands on the same side of town first before heading further out. Make sure your tires are properly inflated to the manufacturer's recommended pressure, and do not drive unnecessary heavy cargo around to give you better gas mileage. If it's not too hot or cold, try to minimize your use of the AC to preserve fuel consumption. If you plan on going somewhere that might be local or within walking distance, try to leave your car at home and go for a walk. It's a good way to get your exercise in while saving money on gas. Cutting down corners here and there can add up and help save money and, in the long run, can help you become better at money management.

If you have belongings at home, such as an old TV, shoes, or clothes that you no longer use or need, try selling them. The more unnecessary things you can get rid of from your house, the more decluttered your home will be, which can be beneficial in many ways. A less cluttered house can help reduce stress and help you become more efficient. You will spend less time looking for things when your home is decluttered. Additionally, you may earn a few extra dollars in your pocket by selling anything you no longer need.

When you are not working, there are a lot of things that you can do that do not need to involve money or at least not a lot of money. A good example is hanging out at the park or beach. You can de-stress for free in nature and breathing the air outside can help refresh you. If you want to visit a museum, research the days that may be free or discounted. Most museums I know offer one free day a month to local residents. If you have kids, you can take them to participate in free workshops or events at the library, church, or Home Depot. Find out when the free events are happening. There are a lot of things that you can do for free. On the other hand, if you prefer to hang out at home, there are also plenty of things you can do, such as working out, watching some inspirational videos, listening to your favorite music, dancing, or singing your heart out.

Take it one day at a time. Keep working and keep on moving forward with life. Don't think about the past because the past is gone, and you cannot go back to correct it. What you can do is focus on the future. So set up new goals and make them achievable with small steps. Start over by living a more conservative lifestyle and not expect to live the way you did before. Create your new budget, throw out any unnecessary expenses and stick to it. You can revise it as your financial situation improves.

If you have children that will be attending college, see if they can apply for financial aid and scholarships. If for some reason, the student is denied financial aid or scholarships, the student can apply for loans under his or her name. Given the circumstances that you are in, it is understandable to gently place the financial responsibility on the child. As the child is transitioning into an adult now, he or she can learn the responsibility of borrowing money and working his or her way to pay back the loans. You cannot baby the child for the rest of his or her life, so this can be a good starting point to hand over financial responsibility. If the loan is too much for the child to handle, then consider applying or transferring to a more affordable college. Many states are now offering tuition-free community colleges.

| EMOTIONAL HEALING

"Life is 10% what happens to you and 90% how you react to it."
— Charles R. Swindoll

For anyone who is finding themselves struggling to heal emotionally, please read on. I hope you will become a renewed person after reading this chapter.

To begin the emotional healing process, you first must understand that you are only human. As humans, we are not perfect. We all have our strengths, but we also have our weaknesses, and we will all make some mistakes from time to time. And at some point in our lives, we will all eventually face adversities, trials, and tribulations. But how we respond to our mistakes, adversities, trials, and tribulations will either make us or break us. We will either learn from them and grow stronger and more resilient, or we can fall apart. I would say it would be more favorable if you could see past your human weakness, learn from your mistakes, and put up a good fight to overcome any misfortunes or adversities you will face. To not learn is almost synonymous with not living, which is probably not what we were intended to be put on this earth for. I believe we were put on this earth to live life to the fullest, even in the face of adversities, trials, and tribulations.

As a result of the scam, it is understandably natural for you to feel angry, betrayed, sad, hurt, and devastated due to the chain of events that led to your loss. You've also understandably lost trust, experienced depression, and lost almost all hope. You've faced the roller-coaster of emotions and regularly relived the original events, which worsens your mood swings and interferes with your ability to concentrate. You've been living through the pain and, at some points, had suicidal thoughts. You feel regretful because the damage has been done, the time has gone, and there is nothing you can do to turn back the clock. You have hit rock bottom.

You look back and now realize all the red flags you weren't aware of before. You feel stupid. You feel naïve. You wished you could turn back the clock to reverse everything. However, as we all know, the clock cannot be turned back, no matter how hard we wish. Regardless of what has happened and how you feel, life will go on. So, what will you do now? What will be the plan?

Understanding that not everything in life will happen the way we may want or intend them to and that there may be, along the way, an unfortunate chain of events that may knock us down to the ground, we have the power to decide what we should do in the event these unexpected and unfortunate circumstances do happen to us. As with other victims of the PBS scam, our banks are completely emptied, and our hearts are shattered. We are severely broken financially and emotionally. In other words, we got hit by a double whammy. Isn't that completely insane?! The question is, what will you do now? How do you overcome this devastation?

Knowing that there is absolutely nothing that we can do to turn back the clock and that time will go on whether or not we spend it wisely, we must do what we can to get back up on our feet and fight for what we believe in. We must acknowledge the situation we are in, accept and face the truth that the unthinkable has happened, and experience and grow through the pain of the trauma, but we will use that pain and take the opportunity to strengthen ourselves. Maybe this new problem we got ourselves into is a wake-up call to see the bigger picture? What is our purpose on this earth? What role should we take moving forward? This is a time to reflect on your strengths, work on your weakness and have faith that you can pull yourself out of every situation. Meditate, pray, connect with your spiritual energy, and believe in and trust the universe.

Why not turn that feeling of hopelessness around and say, "hey, I still have a future ahead of me that I can write," and "Despite my loss which does not and will not define me, I can and will make the best of all the years to come." How about making a positive change for a better future by accepting and taking the lessons you have learned from past mistakes? It doesn't matter if your mistakes were from your own doing or as a result of the persuasion of another human being. Once mistakes are made, they are meant to teach you a lesson and how to grow stronger. The money you have lost should not define you, nor should the opinion or acts of another person. Your happiness should also never be defined by anyone or anything else.

Have you ever noticed why some people are always happy and why others never seem to be happy? Or why are some people rich and others poor? It is not because they are born a certain way or have a certain advantage over others. The truth behind their happiness and wealth is almost always a result of one thing: CHOICE. Happy people are not always happy because bad things don't happen to them. That is far from the truth. It is

THE PIG BUTCHERING SCAM

because they choose to be happy. They choose to let go of the negative things in their life. They choose to forgive, and they choose to look at the positive side of life and focus on the good things. They choose to see the cup as half full and fill the rest up with wine. They choose to be grateful even in the face of adversity. Similarly, not all wealthy people were born wealthy. There are many wealthy people that come from extremely poor families and grew up in severe poverty. However, it is the choice in life that they make that has led them to become wealthy. They've learned to value and save money. They learned to make many sacrifices, cut out or delay instant gratification, and learned how to make long-term decisions.

Starting today, you can choose the person you want to become. You do not need to let the past define who you are today or tomorrow. You may have lost all your money or landed in debt, and you may have lost some people along the way that you thought were your friends. Maybe you even lost the trust from your spouse or significant other due to the misunderstanding of unfathomable events that led to your loss, or maybe you've even gotten divorced as a result. But you cannot tie your self-worth or self-esteem to your loss or your spouse's misunderstanding. You just cannot do that. Today, you can either choose to be your own best friend or your own worst enemy. I would say here it would be more favorable to pick the first option. You can choose to learn to love yourself. You can choose to be kind to yourself. You can choose not to be a prisoner of your past.

As Abraham Lincoln's timeless advice goes, "this too shall pass." Just know that no matter how hard it is now, it will not always be this way. The opposite can also be applied to this saying. If things are good, remember it won't always be this way as well. So, with the good days, enjoy every great moment and for the bad times, take it one day at a time. Understand that there is a time and place for everything. We will grieve when unfortunate events happen. For some, it may take a lot longer than others. However, life goes on, and we simply cannot stay stagnant in one place forever. We must learn to adapt to changes, even if they are unfavorable, and make some lemonade when life gives us lemons. We must learn from our mistakes, and we must learn not to let anyone or anything define us. Just trust and give in to the universe. Life is short, and we should live it the way it's meant to be lived. So, pick yourself up and keep pushing forward. Also, remember that whatever you may be going through, another person has probably already gone through it or is going through a similar situation as you are reading this book right now. There is always going to be someone who may be in a worse position than you. The best way to live life is simply to be grateful. Whether it is for the air we breathe, the food we have access to, the roof over our head, or family who loves us unconditionally, being grateful can help you heal and move forward better.

All we need to do now is take baby steps, work on one small thing one day at a time and see results down the line. The healing process will take time, but you will eventually come to a place where you feel you can be proud of yourself and that you've accomplished so much. For me, I am simply grateful that I have my health and can work to rebuild over time what I have lost. I am also grateful my family loves me no matter what I go through.

I am grateful for understanding that even though I have made my costly mistakes, I am still not a failure. I know I have a lot to learn, and I will become a stronger person by persevering through these unprecedented times. Although it has been a difficult journey post-scam, I have learned not to let past events tie me down. I continue to learn from my mistakes. I will not dwell on the past or worry about tomorrow. I will focus on today and the baby steps I need to make a better tomorrow. I will tackle one difficulty at a time. I will take everything slowly and not expect rapid results. I will not try to overdo anything or over-extend myself. I know my limits and will set healthy boundaries. I will set aside at least a few minutes every day to do something that I enjoy and will replenish my energy. I will learn to find confidence and trust again. I will accept what has happened to me and the things that I cannot control. I will stay calm, react positively, and continue to be grateful for many things in my life. Most importantly, I will remember that I am worthy and deserve to love myself the best that I can.

YOU WILL BECOME STRONGER

To all the victims of financial or investment scams out there, know that with our remaining time on earth, we can eventually make our money back as long as we have our health. We must focus on our health and treat it like gold. Gold, as everyone knows it, is a very precious commodity. So, learn to maintain your health by learning how to manage your emotions and thoughts. Focus on what you can control, and don't waste energy on things that you cannot. Do not let the scammers take any more control of your life. Get out of that hamster wheel you may have found yourself circling and trapped in. Stop reliving the events that brought you to where you are but instead focus your energy on what you can do and what actions you can take. Do not allow any more people or circumstances to control your life. You are in charge of your life, so regain it by focusing on positive thoughts. Learn positive affirmations.

Disengage yourself from all forms of negativity, including the thought of blaming. Stop blaming yourself and stop blaming others because doing so is fruitless. Instead, build new boundaries, make changes, and learn to smile again. It may, on the surface, sound quite strange and insensitive to say this here, but I will share it anyways. I heard it through the grapevine that laughter can be the best medicine! It may seem like a long time ago that you had laughed but today is a new day. Embrace it. You have a lot to live for. With a positive mindset, self-care, and proper emotional support, you will have the courage and resilience to persevere to become a stronger person you never thought would be possible. So let go of your worries as worrying will not solve anything, but plan and focus on actions that you can take to help you recover and move on with life.

In the remainder of this chapter, I would like to share steps that you can take to help with the recovery and healing process. There are many things you can do to take your mind off the pain and hurt. While some methods may help one person, you might find a different method that may help you heal and recover better.

First step: Take care of your body

Remember, your health is a precious commodity, so do not let anyone take that away from you. Also, remember that time, too, is a precious commodity. So do not let the scammers drain any more of your time or health. Learn to take care of your body and mind before anything else. Even if you have no appetite, you must make an effort to eat. Eat anything, even if you do not feel like it. As each day or week passes, start to focus on eating healthier. Also, make sure you keep yourself hydrated. Drink water or anything that makes you feel good to regain your health and energy. The regained energy will allow you to think and function better.

Second: make sure you get enough sleep. The entire post-scam experience can take a toll on the quality of sleep due to the severe stress and anxiety, making it more difficult to fall asleep and, for some, having nightmares during sleep. Try to establish a relaxing routine before going to bed. Take a warm bath, read a motivational book, or listen to some positive affirmations to help you fall asleep and gently remove some negative thoughts. If you have a hard time falling asleep, try taking an over-the-counter supplement called Melatonin. Or, you can also try an herb or supplement called Valerian Root, which is known for its calming benefits and helps promote the length and quality of restorative sleep. If these supplements do not help, and anxiety is keeping you up, see if your doctor can prescribe an anti-anxiety medication to help you relax at night and get a better night's sleep. If you are suffering from depression, your doctor may prescribe you an antidepressant which can also help you sleep. If you fall asleep but are awakened in the middle of the night, your doctor can prescribe medications to help maintain your sleep. Alternatively, you can try an over-the-counter sleep aid such as Unisom to keep you well-rested throughout the night. Make sure you double-check with your doctor or pharmacist about the appropriate dosage and any potential drug-drug interactions with other medications you may already be taking.

Two: Join a support group

Most support groups are free. Find a group that is more specific for trauma or crime victims. You will feel less lonely and isolated and know that you really are not struggling alone. Facebook or other online platforms may have support groups, but you must be extra cautious of any potential scammers lurking there.

GASO support group was created especially for PBS victims and will only allow victims through a vetted process to exclude potential scammers from joining. You will feel more welcomed and understood in this group where people have been in your shoes or are currently in a similar situation. It costs no money to join this group.

Other support groups out there that you can consider:

Mental Health America's Support Group:
https://www.mhnational.org/find-support-groups

National Alliance on Mental Illness Support Group:
https://www.nami.org/support-education/support-groups

Sharing your story will not only relieve you of the burden and stress you hold inside, but it can also benefit the listener. Furthermore, telling someone your account will not only benefit the listener because they are now aware of the scam and hence will be less likely to fall for them, but they can also help spread awareness and be vigilant and protective of the people they care for. Therefore, sharing your knowledge and experience is important in protecting others against scams.

You can talk openly and honestly about your experience without being unfairly judged, which may help decrease your stress, depression, and anxiety.

From talking and listening to others who have gone through a similar experience as you, you might pick up new skills and learn how to cope better with the challenges you face.

Three: Get your blood pumping

Find things to do to get your mind off the trauma. Do things that are enjoyable, and that can help you replenish your energy.

Anything that you can do to get your blood pumping will be physically and mentally beneficial. Studies have shown that exercise can help improve mood because it releases endorphins which are also known as "feel-good" hormones. Exercising can increase your heart rate, which triggers norepinephrine, a chemical in the brain shown to help with stress.

A good starting point may be a walk in the park, whether it be alone, with a friend, or with a pet.

Jogging is great if you are physically able to do it, so as long as you do not have any joint or foot pain or any other reason to prevent yourself from doing so.

Ride a stationary bike or ride outside to feel the breeze flowing across your face.

Try boxing or playing tennis to release all the tension and anger from your system.

Lift weights and do push up or squats to help improve your circulation.

Dance to your favorite song or workout music.

Do anything that can bring you joy!

Four: Relax

It is great to get a balance of exercise and relaxing time.

Watch a movie that lifts your mood, something funny or inspirational.

Read a book, especially an inspirational one.

Draw or paint.

Do some gardening.

Walk or play with pets.

Work on puzzles.

Go to church. Aside increasing your spirituality and finding peace, going to church can help reduce stress, anxiety, and depression.

Clean up your room or house. Not only does cleaning your home help kill germs which can also help prevent or reduce allergy symptoms, but studies have shown that clean space can also make you feel calmer, helps lower stress and anxiety, and improves focus.

Listen to your favorite music. I always find comfort in listening to music. There is a variety of music that comforts me, including trance, because it seems to take me away into another world which I find, for the time being, takes my mind away from the pain. Overall, music uplifts me every time I listen to it. You can also benefit from listening to meditation music as its calming effects can help you to relax, reduce stress or anxiety and promote better sleep.

Sing along to your favorite music.

Write a journal. I find it extremely helpful to write all my thoughts down, so it does not get bottled up inside. I feel like my soul has been freed once I have written out my thoughts, and I feel a great sense of relief. Even if it brings back temporary memories of the trauma I went through, I feel like I am one step closer to moving forward with my life by releasing that burden off my chest onto something else. And although it took me over a year to finally share my experience with you, I feel relieved and very therapeutic to have shared my story and written this book.

Five: Meditate or Pray

Learn to master your emotions. You can do many things that can help improve your emotional well-being and bring in a sense of calmness, peace, and balance.

Meditate. Meditation can help you in many ways, including staying centered, increasing self-awareness, and promoting inner peace. It can also help reduce brain chatter and improve focus. Overactive brain chatter has been tied to negative health issues such as depression or heart problems. Try not to overthink everything. Fear and worry do not solve anything but only take away today's joy and rob us of our peace. So learn to silence or divert negative thoughts through the practice of meditation. I have found a website[2] that can help guide you to meditate: *https://www.mindful.org/how-to-meditate/*.

Do some yoga. Yoga also has many benefits, including increasing mindfulness and reducing stress and anxiety. You can follow some yoga activities on this helpful website[3] I found:

https://www.hopkinsmedicine.org/health/wellness-and-prevention/9-benefits-of-yoga.

Go outdoors, get fresh air and practice deep breathing. Learn to let everything go.

Pray. When you pray, you can feel a sense of connection to a higher power and grow stronger in spirit. Praying can help release any burden or pain you carry alone on your shoulders to the higher power that you confide in. It will, in turn, reduce your feelings of fear, loneliness, or isolation. Because the act of praying can calm you down, it can also help build your inner strength, reduce your stress, and help you go through life's most challenging times.

Do nothing, or soak in a bit of sun. This is one of my favorite things to do. I enjoy sitting or lying in the hammock in my backyard, cherish the sun's warmth, and just do nothing. I feel happy and at peace when I am relaxing in the sun for just a few minutes. There are many benefits to getting enough sunlight. When exposed to enough sunlight, which generally can average to around 10-15min per day depending on your skin type, your body can produce enough Vitamin D. Wearing sunscreen may interfere with your body producing sufficient amounts. Most people know that Vitamin D can strengthen your bones and regulate your immune system. But enough Vitamin D can also help reduce blood pressure, improve sleep quality, and help boost your mood, which means it can also help fight off depression.

Six: Forgive

Forgiving can have benefits too. There's the saying "forgive and forget," but no matter how hard I try, I feel that I will never be able to forget. So, I will not attempt to persuade you to forget the past. I will try, however, to encourage you to let go and not focus on the past. Instead, learn to forgive the person that had wronged and hurt you.

One thing that some people may not understand about forgiveness is that you are not doing anyone else a favor. Instead, you would be the beneficiary of the act of forgiving. Studies have shown that forgiving can help you heal because you will release all the negative feelings that drain your mind and body, and eventually, you will find a sense of peace and strength from within.

One of the great things about forgiving someone is that you are freeing the control that person had on you all along. It does not mean that you are condoning their harmful actions but that you have decided to make peace with the pain that had been inflicted on you and that you are finally ready to let it go. Once you let go, you will finally be able to release the victim mentality that may have been an obstacle in your recovery process. Once you remove the mindset of being stuck as a forever victim, your mind will be set free, and you will be able to move on more gracefully to the next chapter of your life.

When you choose not to forgive, you are choosing to place yourself back in a prison cell of bitterness and poison. While ironically, you might want revenge or wish the person who had harmed you dies, it is you who will be drinking your own poison. That is because the other person may have no idea how you are feeling years after the scam and has long moved on with his or her life, or maybe the other person has already died from whatever reason. However, it is you who are still holding grudges and hence suffering and drowning in your own pool of pain and bitterness.

It may be hard to forgive others if you do not know how to forgive yourself. Remember, the past mistakes you have made or the wrongdoing of another person does not define you. You are human, and you are worthy. Forgiving yourself will free you from your past and the burdens you have been carrying. Use your experience as a learning opportunity for growth in your spiritual and life journey.

Once I learned to forgive myself because I understand that as a human being, I am prone to making mistakes but also, at the same time, the crime that was committed against me was not my fault, I have come to peace with myself and eventually learned to also forgive my scammer. I have learned that although the scammers have mastered their techniques of psychological manipulation and persuasion by exploiting my weakness of trusting others, that on the other side is also another human being. This other human being is also capable of being manipulated and exploited to commit the fraud that he or she had carried out. The lesson that should be learned is that forgiving is an essential part of the healing process, but you must continually educate yourself to prevent falling for another scam.

Seven: Help others

There are many things you can do to help people that require no money but only your time. But only do this when you have reached a point where you can get enough sleep, regain enough strength through self-care, and have the energy to function.

You can volunteer your time to help those in need. It can help you to think less about the stress in your life and more about how you are alleviating hardships that other people are also facing.

Helping others can strengthen your bonds or connections with others and bring value to those around you, which will give you a sense of accomplishment. It is also a great way to lift your mood by showing gratitude for the good things in your life.

Even if you are not happy at the present moment, at least you know you will make a difference in someone else's life because you will make people feel cared for and loved.

These are a few ways that you can help others:

Volunteer at your local church, school, or charity.

Babysit or volunteer at a nursing home.

Do grocery shopping or yardwork for a family, friend, or neighbor.

Donate old clothing, shoes, toys, and things you no longer need.

Share your knowledge and skills, such as language or computer, with organizations.

Read a story to kids at the local library or tutor a student who cannot afford private lessons whenever you can.

Be a good listener to a friend in need or an elderly person who has no one to talk to.

Pray for people who are also in the midst of their own crises or experiencing problems.

Eight: Learn to laugh

Although laughing may not entirely take away your pain, it can help with the healing and recovery process. After the discovery of being scammed, this is probably the very last thing a scam survivor would feel or imagine ever doing again. This is quite understandable, as severe stress may hinder you from the thought of ever laughing again. But throughout history, there seems to be a consensus that laughter is the best medicine, and many studies have shown the beneficial effects of laughter.

First of all, if you are laughing, you probably will not feel anxious, angry, or sad at the moment. Laughing can trigger healthy physical and emotional responses in your body, such as improving your mood and reducing trauma-induced tensions, diminishing your pain, and strengthening your immune system.

According to the Psychiatric Times, happiness and humor can improve brain function due to increased connectivity in various parts of the brain in response to laughter.[4] Humor and laughter can have calming effects and help break the cycle between pain, sleep loss, depression, and immunosuppression. Other benefits can include lowering blood pressure and glucose and improving the defense against respiratory infections. Due to their benefits, we should make our life experiences as positive as we can through laughter and humor.

Humor and laughter can also help lift your burdens, inspire hope and help you release your anger and forgive sooner.

So go out and watch a funny movie or sitcom or hang out with friends who know how to have humor.

Read a joke book or interact with young kids. Most children I know are natural-born comedians and can give you a good free laugh. I know my kids do. See, the best things in life are free.

So go out and make it a resolution to laugh more.

Nine: Set new goals

Set new goals that are meaningful.
Set new boundaries.
Rebuild from scratch.

Ten: Practice Positive Affirmations every day for healing

Learn the law of attraction. Focus your energy on positive thoughts to bring positive results to your life and avoid negative thoughts as they may bring negative outcomes.

Use the power of your own thoughts to find peace and reach acceptances.

Write down things that you are grateful for and focus on happy moments.

Practice positive affirmations to help heal trauma.

Rehearse these lines every day until they're engrained in your heart, mind, and soul:

1. My past does not define my present and will not define my future.
2. I let go of my past to embrace my future.
3. I will not let people who have wronged me control my future.
4. I will not hold a grudge against people who have wronged me in the past, for holding a grudge will only drain me of my strength.
5. I will not waste time or energy on past regrets.
6. I will always remember to forgive myself and others that have hurt me in the past.
7. I will not allow other people to define my health.
8. I am happy to let my body heal at its own pace and its own way.
9. I will be gentle with myself in allowing myself to heal.
10. I do not try to deny the discomfort and pain that I feel.
11. I am more than the sum of my injuries and trauma.
12. I will focus on positive things and positive energy.
13. I will treat myself with love and caring.
14. I will never feel guilty about taking time for self-healing.
15. I will learn to laugh again because I know it can benefit me in many ways.

Rehearsing and engraining these positive affirmations in my heart, mind, and soul have a calming and soothing effect on me, and I feel like a renewed person. I hope you feel the same way too and have benefited from most of the lessons that I have shared in this chapter.

If all else fails: Seek professional help if doing any of the above has not helped

After many months post-scam, what once felt like the end of the world should now feel like life with a new beginning. When you once felt like screaming at the top of your lungs, you now feel more at peace. I hope you have learned to forgive yourself. I hope you have learned to love and embrace yourself.

However, if you feel nothing has worked or still find that your emotions are not controllable and it is difficult to move on, please seek professional help.

You can seek help from a psychologist, psychiatrist, or cognitive behavior therapist who has experience with trauma or crisis therapy.

Psychiatrists are licensed doctors who diagnose and treat a wide range of mental illnesses. If you still suffer from depression, severe anxiety, suicidal thoughts, eating disorders, and/or continued insomnia as a result of post scam, a psychiatrist may prescribe meds that can help alter and improve your mood or help calm you down or give professional advice on how to handle your unsettling emotions. They can also use psychotherapy or neuromodulation. The important thing is they are experts trained to listen and work with you and will come up with a personal treatment plan that they feel will be best for you.

Psychologists can help people learn to cope with stressful situations, overcome addictions, and manage their chronic illnesses. They do tests and assessments that can help diagnose disorders or analyze the way a person thinks, feels, and behaves. In other words, they identify psychological, emotional, behavioral, and organizational issues. Psychologists utilize psychotherapy, also known as talk therapy, as their roadmap. Common types of therapy they use include cognitive-behavioral, interpersonal, psychoanalysis, or psychodynamic. However, psychologists do not prescribe medications.

Cognitive Behavioral Therapy (CBT) is usually conducted by a psychiatrist, psychologist, mental health nurse, or general practitioner. CBT usually focuses on your current problems rather than issues from your past. Its primary focus is to help you gain control of your thoughts. It can help you raise your self-esteem, manage your anger, and improve your communication skills and positive thoughts.

Some online mental health platforms can also provide mental health services, including counseling and therapy. Although there are plenty of platforms that may exist, it is hard to say which might work best for each individual. However, I have heard positive feedback on a platform called "Better Help," as they may be able to pair you up with a trauma specialist in a timely matter, usually within a few days. These specialists are licensed and have a Master's or Doctorate degree. Using this platform may yield quicker responses and results than if you were to use your insurance and have to wait a long time before seeing anyone. The platform allows you to chat online or through video appointments. You can also communicate via phone or text. The price may be a little steep for someone who has just lost all their money, but if you can afford it for the short term, it may help pull you through the crisis until you are able to see a regular therapist through your insurance. You can access their platform and learn more by visiting: *https://www.betterhelp.com/.*

CONCLUSION

"IT CAN NEVER HAPPEN TO ME"

So, that is what I had thought, before I got scammed. And that is what every victim I knew had also thought. Until one becomes a victim, the universal myth is: "I will never be scammed" as "I am a cautious or careful person," and therefore, the risk of "me" getting scammed is low. The belief that because one is cautious and educated, one will never be deceived or scammed, has been proven over and over to be untrue. Sadly, every victim who has fallen prey has learned the hard lesson that being scammed can happen to anyone. Even the most intelligent, cautious, and financially responsible people have fallen victim to the PBS.

After reading about the effects of ill-intentioned psychological manipulation and persuasion, you should have a better understanding of why no one is fully immune to being scammed. Scammers leverage the universal human belief that we are all too smart and well-educated to be manipulated by criminals. Despite how educated or innately intelligent you are, and staying on top of all the current types of scams, it is impossible to predict and prepare for every possible scam. It simply cannot be emphasized enough that everyone is susceptible. As Jason Tower, an executive at the United States Institute of Peace, stated in reference to the human trafficking atrocities of the PBS, "The criminals are limited only by their imagination."[1]

If you feel that you are above being persuaded and think it cannot happen to you, you should reconsider. It can happen anytime you let your guard down. Though you may think you know it all, the criminals in the cyber scam industry are always trying to stay ahead of you. They will continually learn about how you live, how you think, and your weaknesses and will use society's progress and advancement to their advantage. They are continually following news and events and studying our thought processes until they can find a way to manipulate our thoughts and emotions. So never let yourself get caught off guard. Always watch your back and be wary of new friends who present themselves as helpers.

BE VIGILANT

If Something Sounds Too Good to Be True, It Probably Is

We have all heard the adage, "If something sounds too good to be true, it probably is." As pessimistic as it sounds, this warning should be taken to heart when it comes to investing. My approach post-scam is to be suspicious of everyone and everything until proven innocent, true, or vetted by a trusted family or organization. I would say forget about all the hype you've been hearing about crypto since 2017, which has only increased since. Crypto ads were seen everywhere, promoted by famous people, and even a major stadium in Los Angeles was named after Crypto.com. Let's pull ourselves together, open our eyes, look again, and see what is truly happening. Sure, there are some legitimate crypto websites and exchanges, but due to the weak laws or security protocols and bugs in code, cryptocurrency has truly become a breeding ground for criminal activity. As many victims in our group have observed, crypto exchanges are ideal for criminals. Unlike credit cards, crypto transactions are irreversible. Therefore, consumers must be very suspicious of crypto transactions. If you venture into crypto, only invest in what you can afford to lose. If you are unsure if the crypto or mining pool website you plan on doing your trading with is legitimate, you can look up the IP address with this website: *https://whoisdog.com*. Make sure to never transfer funds to unknown addresses.

Keep yourself up to date on the new types of scams. Go to the FBI, FTC, CFTC, BBB, and other government websites and read their alerts about scams and the latest scams going around. When you educate yourself, you can make better decisions and proceed with caution if something looks off. Being vigilant will help prevent us from falling victim to scams, especially in our retirement years. If you've been scammed once, learn to protect yourself from future occurrences. Scammers are hiding everywhere, waiting for you to seek their "help."

When in doubt, trust your gut and keep doing research. Never proceed with any investments or offers that seem too good to be true. And never automatically trust someone who claims to have experience with investment unless you know them personally and they have helped you out with other little things before. Learn how scammers use social engineering and psychological manipulation to avoid falling into their traps. By learning the psychological manipulation techniques that scammers use to control your mind, you will be more prepared to turn off your automatic reaction when appropriate.

Reexamine your thoughts and how you would typically react to someone and be more vigilant and not automatically willing to help others, especially if you have never met them in person. Unfortunately, victims are also scammed by criminals they met in person.

It may be wise to assume a person you have never met before who is trying to help you, whether in person or online, is a scammer. I used to give people the benefit of the doubt and trusted easily. Now, I will see someone as a scammer until proven genuine. Well, that is my take, but the minimum you should do is always be vigilant and keep educating yourself. Never stop educating yourself. Otherwise, the scammer will win. Learn to say "no" and avoid anything you are unsure of.

BE COMPASSIONATE

Do not traumatize victims any further. Remind victims that they are not "dumb" and help them focus on what they can do. Anyone, at any IQ level, can be scammed because the effectiveness of mind control is *not* dependent on intelligence.

Understand that scammed victims are not "greedy" but have made the costly mistake of believing in the good of another human being who has coerced them into learning to use an investment tool that they had every reason to believe was legitimate. Unfortunately, most PBS victims thought they would be going into an investment for the benefit of their loved ones. Being scammed is not a sign of weakness, but of humanity. Be careful not to blame the victim for becoming prey, but instead take the time to listen to their story without judgment. There is no need for society to judge and put other human beings down. It would be more constructive if people listened rather than judged. And be careful with how you use the word "greed" because it can damage the psychological well-being of victims and does not help with the recovery process.

Not only do victims face financial and psychological trauma from their perpetrators, but they also deal with shame, embarrassment, and humiliation from society. Victim shaming is unnecessary, but common. We all should learn to be more compassionate, encouraging, and supportive. For the victims' family, friends, acquaintances, and colleagues, this is a reminder to be more understanding of their situation. Listen to them without judgment, focus on assisting in any way you can and encourage them to move forward.

For anyone who has become a victim of the PBS, know that there are resources available and that there is a path to recovery. Never let other people determine your fate. You can control the future and you are worthy. Don't forget that!

| HELP SPREAD AWARENESS

What I want more than anything from writing this book is to spread awareness and help in the fight to bring justice for the PBS and human trafficked victims. Keeping our scam experience a secret will not do any justice for new generations since each generation may be lured in through the same, ill-intentioned use of psychological manipulation and persuasion. I wish that someone had talked to me about the PBS so I would have seen the red flags before being drawn in and losing my life savings. Please make every effort to educate your kids or young siblings, nieces, and nephews. Since children go online frequently in this day and age, they may be most vulnerable due to not having been educated. Teach them how to spot scams and let them know it usually starts with a two-way conversation. They need to learn the basics of never sharing any personal information with anyone, whether through email, text, chat, or other forms of online communication. Most importantly, educate your kids on the dangers of social media. That is where the majority of scams occur.

To true journalists like Cyrus Farivar, Alastair McCready, and Cezary Podkul, keep up the excellent job in investigating, detailing real events, and shedding light on the truth that needs to be spread around the world. Your journalism will bring awareness and continue to help in the fight against human trafficking. With your reporting and exposure, you have already helped many victims of human trafficking to get rescued.

If you have found this book helpful, please share it with a loved one, family, friend, or colleague and invite them to join us in this crusade against crime by further spreading awareness!

Lastly, if you have enjoyed reading this book, kindly leave a review. If you feel it can improve or would like to provide feedback, please send your thoughts to: thePBS2021@gmail.com.

REFERENCES

Introduction

1. FBI Houston Media Office, "$1 billion in losses reported by victims of romance scams," FBI Houston, February 10, 2022. https://www.fbi.gov/contact-us/field-offices/houston/news/press-releases/1-billion-in-losses-reported-by-victims-of-romance-scams

2. Greed. In Merriam-Webster's online dictionary (11th ed.). https://www.merriam-webster.com/dictionary/greed

3. Cezary Podkul, "Alleged Cambodian pig butchering scam operations raided," ProPublica, October 3, 2022. https://www.propublica.org/article/pig-butchering-scams-raided-cambodia-apple-trafficking

4. Lianne Chia, Cheryl Tan, and Ray Yeh, "Inside the elaborate set-up of a SCAM HQ, staffed by people forced to scam," CNA, October 23, 2022. https://www.channelnewsasia.com/cna-insider/inside-elaborate-set-scam-hq-staffed-people-forced-scam-3018966

Chapter 1

Statistics

1. Alastair McCready, "From Industrial-Scale Scam Centers, Trafficking Victims Are Being Forced to Steal Billions," Vice News, July 13, 2022. https://www.vice.com/en/article/n7zb5d/pig-butchering-scam-cambodia-trafficking
2. "Our Story," Global Anti-Scam Org, https://www.globalantiscam.org/about
3. "Slavery Today is Erected by Cryptocurrency and Social Media," Global Anti-Scam Org, July 3, 2022. https://www.globalantiscam.org/post/slavery-today-is-erected-by-cryptocurrency-and-social-media
4. Emma Fletcher, "Reports of Romance Scams Hit Record Highs in 2021," Federal Trade Commission, February 10, 2022. https://www.ftc.gov/news-events/data-visualizations/data-spotlight/2022/02/reports-romance-scams-hit-record-highs-2021
5. Emma Fletcher, "Reports Show Scammers Cashing in on Crypto Craze," Federal Trade Commission, June 3, 2022. https://www.ftc.gov/news-events/data-visualizations/data-spotlight/2022/06/reports-show-scammers-cashing-crypto-craze
6. "CFPB Publishes New Bulletin Analyzing Rise in Crypto-Asset Complaints," Consumer Financial Protection Bureau, November 10, 2022. https://www.consumerfinance.gov/about-us/newsroom/cfpb-publishes-new-bulletin-analyzing-rise-in-crypto-asset-complaints/
7. "1 in 4 Report Getting Scammed in Dating Platforms!" Global Anti-Scam Org, February 13, 2022.

https://www.globalantiscam.org/post/1-in-4-report-getting-scammed-in-dating-platforms

8. "Financial Fraud Crimes - Financial Fraud Crime Victims," The United States Attorney's Office – District of Alaska, February 5, 2020. https://www.justice.gov/usao-ak/financial-fraud-crimes

9. "Statistics of Crypto-Romance / Pig-Butchering Scam," Global Anti-Scam Org, July 7, 2022. https://www.globalantiscam.org/post/statistics-of-crypto-romance-pig-butchering-scam

10. "Myanmar Scam Companies Put up Firework for Every 500k Scammed!," Global Anti-Scam Org, July 11, 2021. https://www.globalantiscam.org/post/myanmar-scam-companies-put-up-firework-for-every-500k-scammed

The PBS Overview

1. Cezary Podkul, "What's a Pig Butchering Scam? Here's How to Avoid Falling Victim to One," ProPublica, September 19, 2022. https://www.propublica.org/article/whats-a-pig-butchering-scam-heres-how-to-avoid-falling-victim-to-one

2. "The Pig-Butchering Scam," Global Anti-Scam Org, https://www.globalantiscam.org/about

3. "737: Winston Sterzel | Don't Lose Your Bacon in a Pig-Butchering Scam," The Jordan Harbinger Show, October 12, 2022. https://www.jordanharbinger.com/winston-sterzel-dont-lose-your-bacon-in-a-pig-butchering-scam/

4. Robert B. Cialdini, Influence: Science and Practice, 5th ed., Boston: Allyn and Bacon, 2008.

5. Pig-Butchering Scam / Sha Zhu Pan -- photos of training manuals. (2021, May 24). Reddit. https://www.reddit.com/r/Scams/comments/njimju/pigbutchering_scam_sha_zhu_pan_photos_of_training/

6. Cyrus Farivar, "Apple Removes a Trading App Linked to Crypto Scams from the App Store," Forbes, September 26, 2022. https://www.forbes.com/sites/cyrusfarivar/2022/09/26/apple-removes-metatrader-crypto-pig-butchering-scams/?sh=686acbb22e31

7. Wong Shiying, "The Pig-Butchering Scam: Con Artists Who Come for Your Heart and Wallet," The Straits Times, February 20, 2022. https://www.straitstimes.com/singapore/courts-crime/the-pig-butchering-scam-con-artists-who-come-for-your-heart-and-wallet

8. Jason Tower & Priscilla A. Clapp, "Chaos Sparked by Myanmar Coup Fuels Chinese Cross-border Crime," The United States Institute of Peace, April 21, 2021. https://www.usip.org/publications/2021/04/chaos-sparked-myanmar-coup-fuels-chinese-cross-border-crime

9. Cezary Podkul, "Human Trafficking's Newest Abuse: Forcing Victims Into Cyberscamming," ProPublica, September 13, 2022. https://www.propublica.org/article/human-traffickers-force-victims-into-cyberscamming

10. Pierson, D. (2022, November 12). Cybercriminals from China hold thousands captive in Cambodia. Los Angeles Times. https://www.latimes.com/world-nation/story/2022-11-01/i-was-a-slave-up-to-100-000-held-captive-by-chinese-cyber-criminals-in-cambodia

11. Priscilla A. Clapp & Jason Tower, "Myanmar's Criminal Zones: A Growing Threat to Global Security," The United States Institute of Peace, November 9, 2022. https://www.usip.org/publications/2022/11/myanmars-criminal-zones-growing-threat-global-security

12. "Google Translate Now Converts Chinese Into English with Neural Machine Translation," VentureBeat, September 27, 2016. https://venturebeat.com/business/google-translate-now-converts-english-into-chinese-with-neural-machine-translation/

13. Al Jazeera English. (2022, July 15). Forced to Scam: Cambodia's Cyber Slaves | 101 East Documentary. YouTube. https://www.youtube.com/watch?v=n-EtdC4zQso

Personal Story

1. NBOX teaches you to borrow a chicken to make eggs - NBOX. (2022, January 6). Medium. https://medium.com/@nboxglobal/nbox-teaches-you-to-borrow-a-chicken-to-make-eggs-cb5b37a1c3bb

SC's Story

1. Channel, D. –. T. D. (2021, December 20). Denver man loses $1.6 million in new "Pig Butchering" cryptocurrency scam. YouTube. https://www.youtube.com/watch?v=5RBiRF8gt44&feature=youtu.be

Cy's Story

1. Brian Quarmby, "'Pig Slaughtering' Crypto Scams Reap Millions on Silicon Valley Dating Apps," Cointelegraph, June 3, 2022. https://cointelegraph.com/news/pig-slaughtering-crypto-scams-reap-millions-on-silicon-valley-dating-apps

2. Cezary Podkul, "What's a Pig Butchering Scam? Here's How to Avoid Falling Victim to One," ProPublica, September 19, 2022. https://www.propublica.org/article/whats-a-pig-butchering-scam-heres-how-to-avoid-falling-victim-to-one

3. ProPublica. (2022, September 20). How Pig Butchering Scams Work. https://www.propublica.org/article/whats-a-pig-butchering-scam-heres-how-to-avoid-falling-victim-to-one

4. Cyrus Farivar, "Innovation Cryptocurrency Scam Victim Who Lost Over $1 Million To Get Over $100k Back, Prosecutor Says," Forbes, October 22, 2022. https://www.forbes.com/sites/cyrusfarivar/2022/10/22/cryptocurrency-scam-victim-who-lost-over-1-million-to-get-over-100000-back-prosecutor-says/

5. Farivar, C. (2022, July 1). 'Pig Butchering' Crypto Scam Victim To Get Money Back From Binance, Law Enforcement Says. Forbes. https://www.forbes.com/sites/cyrusfarivar/2022/07/01/pig-butchering-crypto-scam-victim-to-get-money-back-from-binance-law-enforcement-says/?sh=2ae8d6285ecd

Psychological Manipulation

1. "Tricking English Translators for ShaZhuPan Scripts," Global Anti-Scam Org., March 24, 2022. https://www.globalantiscam.org/post/tricking-english-translators-for-shazhupan-scripts

2. "Hierarchy System of the Scam Companies for Shazhupan," Global Anti-Scam Org., October 1, 2021. https://www.globalantiscam.org/post/hierarchy-system-of-the-scam-companies-for-shazhupan

3. "Manipulation is Controlled Reality," Open Minds Foundation. https://www.openmindsfoundation.org/coercion-coercive-control/what-is-manipulation/
4. "What is the Anchoring Effect?," Harvard Law School - Program on Negotiation. https://www.pon.harvard.edu/tag/anchoring-effect/
5. Steven Hassan, "Opening Our Minds: Avoiding Abusive Relationships and Authoritarian Groups," Freedom of Mind, September 9, 2021. https://freedomofmind.com/opening-our-minds/
6. Al Jazeera English. (2022, July 15). Forced to Scam: Cambodia's Cyber Slaves | 101 East Documentary. YouTube. https://www.youtube.com/watch?v=n-EtdC4zQso
7. Chia, L. (2022, November 24). Inside the elaborate set-up of a scam HQ, staffed by people forced to scam. CNA. https://www.channelnewsasia.com/cna-insider/inside-elaborate-set-scam-hq-staffed-people-forced-scam-3018966
8. https://www.globalantiscam.org/post/victim-sued-for-exposing-scammers

Chapter 3

Report the crime

1. Cyber Crime. (2022, December 22). Federal Bureau of Investigation. https://www.fbi.gov/investigate/cyber
2. Farivar, C. (2022, July 1). 'Pig Butchering' Crypto Scam Victim To Get Money Back From Binance, Law Enforcement Says. Forbes. https://www.forbes.com/sites/cyrusfarivar/2022/07/01/pig-butchering-crypto-scam-victim-to-get-money-back-from-binance-law-enforcement-says/?sh=2ae8d6285ecd

Chapter 4

Healing and Recovery

1. Cardenas, A. (2020, August 30). Homecoming: A Psychological Thriller About Emotions and Memory. Exploring Your Mind. https://exploringyourmind.com/homecoming-psychological-thriller-emotions-memory/
2. Staff, M. (2022, November 15). How to Meditate. Mindful. https://www.mindful.org/how-to-meditate/
3. *9 Benefits of Yoga*. (2021, August 8). Johns Hopkins Medicine. https://www.hopkinsmedicine.org/health/wellness-and-prevention/9-benefits-of-yoga
4. Khajuria, K., MD. (2020, November 16). Laughter Is the Best Medicine. Psychiatric Times. https://www.psychiatrictimes.com/view/laughter-best-medicine

Conclusion

1. David Pierson, "'I was a slave': Up to 100,000 held captive by Chinese cybercriminals in Cambodia," Los Angeles Times, November 1, 2022. https://www.latimes.com/world-nation/story/2022-11-01/i-was-a-slave-up-to-100-000-held-captive-by-chinese-cyber-criminals-in-cambodia

Additional Reading/Videos

1. CBS Boston. (2022, February 11). I-Team: Woman Warns Others After Losing $2.5M In Cryptocurrency Romance Scam. CBS News. https://www.cbsnews.com/boston/news/fbi-boston-cryptocurrency-romance-scam-investigation/

2. Mornings, C. (2022, February 22). Woman loses $390,000 of inheritance in crypto romance scam. YouTube. https://www.youtube.com/watch?v=zHrzrBYRwBY&feature=youtu.be

3. America, G. M. (n.d.). 2 women speak out after losing money to fraudulent suitors on dating apps. Good Morning America. https://www.goodmorningamerica.com/news/video/women-speak-losing-money-fraudulent-suitors-dating-apps-83038207

4. Journal, T. W. S. (2022, November 2). Pig Butchering: A Texting Scam With a Crypto Twist - The Journal. - WSJ Podcasts. WSJ. https://www.wsj.com/podcasts/the-journal/pig-butchering-a-texting-scam-with-a-crypto-twist/0207dd19-f9f7-4bd0-8da3-6f14828689d9

5. Bailey, D. (2022, April 8). What is pig butchering? A crypto romance scam that cost one woman $8M. The Business of Business. https://www.businessofbusiness.com/articles/pig-butchering-crypto-romance-scam/

6. Fraudulent Recovery Services: How Not to Fall for a Scam Twice. (n.d.). Binance Blog. https://www.binance.com/en/blog/community/fraudulent-recovery-services-how-not-to-fall-for-a-scam-twice-3757133141389741964

7. Lin, S. (2022, February 24). Chinese Fraud Rings Operate Large Internet Scam Firms in Cambodia: Insiders. www.theepochtimes.com. https://www.theepochtimes.com/mkt_app/chinese-fraud-

rings-operate-large-internet-scam-firms-in-cambodia-insiders_4296230.html

8. ProPublica. (2022, October 1). How Human Traffickers Force Victims Into Cyberscamming. https://www.propublica.org/article/human-traffickers-force-victims-into-cyberscamming

9. Xiao, M. (2022, October 7). "Pig butchering" crypto scams spotlight need for an evolution in fraud prevention for finance. SC Media. https://www.scmagazine.com/analysis/security-awareness/pig-butchering-crypto-scams-spotlight-need-for-an-evolution-in-fraud-prevention-for-finance

10. Writer, S. (2021, August 31). Cyber slavery: inside Cambodia's online scam gangs. Nikkei Asia. https://asia.nikkei.com/Spotlight/The-Big-Story/Cyber-slavery-inside-Cambodia-s-online-scam-gangs

11. English, A. J. (2022, July 15). Forced to Scam: Cambodia's Cyber Slaves | 101 East Documentary. YouTube. https://www.youtube.com/watch?v=n-EtdC4zQso&feature=youtu.be

12. Southern, L. K. A. N. P. (2022, August 20). The online scammer targeting you could be trapped in a South-East Asian fraud factory. The Sydney Morning Herald. https://www.smh.com.au/world/asia/the-online-scammer-targeting-you-could-be-trapped-in-a-south-east-asian-fraud-factory-20220818-p5baz3.html

13. Auto, H. (2022, June 22). Malaysian teenager forced to become a scammer after falling for job ad. The Straits Times. https://www.straitstimes.com/singapore/courts-crime/malaysian-teenager-forced-to-become-a-scammer-after-falling-for-job-ad-0

14. Help for Victims of Ponzi Investment Schemes | Internal Revenue Service. (n.d.). https://www.irs.gov/newsroom/help-for-victims-of-ponzi-investment-schemes

www.ingramcontent.com/pod-product-compliance
Lightning Source LLC
Chambersburg PA
CBHW041041050426

42335CB00056B/3195